Agroindustrial Project Analysis

EDI Series in Economic Development

Agroindustrial
Project Analysis

James E. Austin

PUBLISHED FOR
THE ECONOMIC DEVELOPMENT INSTITUTE
OF THE WORLD BANK

The Johns Hopkins University Press
BALTIMORE AND LONDON

Library of Congress Cataloging in Publication Data

Austin, James E
  Agroindustrial project analysis.

  (EDI Series in Economic Development)
  Bibliography: p. 199
  Includes index.
  1. Agricultural industries. I. Title.
II. Series: Washington, D.C. Economic Development Institute
EDI Series in Economic Development
HD9000.5.A97   338.4   80–550
ISBN 0-8018-2412-5
ISBN 0-8018-2413-3 (pbk.)

Contents

Figures

Tables

Foreword

AGROINDUSTRY—that is, industry based on the processing of agricultural raw materials—is of growing importance in the economies of developing countries. In some instances, the processing is required to prepare a primary product for domestic or foreign trade. In others, agroindustry offers a means of increasing the domestic value added of a raw material through manufacture. With rising incomes and growing urbanization in developing countries, the demand for processed foods in particular tends to increase rapidly. Consideration of these issues led the Economic Development Institute in 1974 to initiate courses in agroindustrial projects for planners from the developing world. The present volume grows out of training materials prepared for those courses.

This book is intended to be an applied guide to the design and analysis of agroindustrial investments in developing countries. It should be of use both as a tool for national planners concerned with agroindustry and as a training aid for courses in investment analysis. Those responsible for investments in the agroindustrial sector commonly have backgrounds in either agriculture or industry but not both; this book provides an introduction to the subject that encompasses both areas of expertise. It does assume, however, that the user has a working knowledge of the structure of his country's economy.

This book is one of a number published or in preparation that arise from the training courses of the Economic Development Institute. We hope that making these publications available for wider circulation will assist those new to the field in mastering relevant analytical techniques that can lead to more efficient investment planning.

AJIT MOZOOMDAR
Director, Economic Development Institute
The World Bank

Preface

THE SEEDS OF THIS BOOK were planted in 1973 by Günter Koenig—at that time Division Chief, French and Ibero-American Courses, and currently Regional Coordinator, Latin America and Europe—in the Economic Development Institute (EDI) of the World Bank. EDI had determined that the importance of agroindustries in developing countries warranted increased attention to the unique characteristics of these enterprises within the World Bank's training efforts. Accordingly, Günter was given the responsibility for creating and administering a course on agroindustrial projects for officials of developing countries. I had the privilege of assisting Günter in this undertaking. His experience, intellect, and good humor were essential to the successful creation of the first agroindustrial projects course and its subsequent development.

This book is an outgrowth of that course development and would not have been possible without the continual encouragement and insights of Günter. I express my deepest appreciation for his support and friendship and hope that this book does justice to his efforts. Price Gittinger, currently Coordinator of Training Materials and Publications at EDI, also provided critical support for our efforts to produce a book that would contribute to the educational activities of the international development community.

Our original concepts and materials underwent an iterative process of refinement to increase their utility for agroindustrial project analysts in developing countries. They were tested over several years in many different courses held both in Washington and in developing countries. Furthermore, the concepts and methodology have been applied by various government officials in formulating strategies for agroindustrial development and in analyzing agroindustrial projects. The comments and suggestions of these hundreds of colleagues from developing countries were invaluable in our tailoring the materials to the realities and needs of the developing countries.

The following colleagues gave generously of their time to reading drafts of the manuscript and provided extremely useful comments: Walter Falcon, Stanford University Food Research Institute; Ray Goldberg, Louis Wells, and George Lodge of the Harvard University Graduate School of Business Administration; Robert Youker, Price Gittinger, and Günter Koenig of EDI; Nancy Barry, World Bank; Kenneth Hoadley, Instituto Panamericano de Alta Dirección de Empresas; Primitivo Zepeda Salazar, Banco de México, Gustavo Esteva, Comité Promotor de Investigaciones para el Desarrollo Rural; and Ferruccio Accame, Jaime Romero, Frank Meissner, and Hugh Swartz of the Inter-American Development Bank. Samuel Yong, formerly of the Massachusetts Institute of Technology, provided invaluable research assistance in analyzing the food technology aspects of the book.

This book would not have been possible without the support of three institutions. The World Bank's EDI and the Training Division of the Inter-American Development Bank jointly sponsored the original courses in agroindustrial project analysis and the subsequent development of the teaching materials. The Division of Research of the Harvard University Graduate School of Business Administration also provided support that enabled my finishing the manuscript.

My thanks also go to Sara Hazel, Beverly Vidler, and Rose Giacobbe and her staff, who patiently and carefully typed and retyped the manuscript's many drafts. James E. McEuen edited the manuscript for publication. Raphael Blow prepared the charts, Christine Houle and Brian J. Svikhart managed production of the book, Chris Jerome read and corrected proof, and Ralph Ward and James Silvan indexed the text.

To all of these individuals I express my warmest thanks. It is my hope that our collective effort will contribute to the development of more efficient, effective, and equitable agroindustrial projects in the developing world.

JAMES E. AUSTIN

Agroindustrial
Project Analysis

1

An Overview

THE PURPOSE OF THIS BOOK is to provide and illustrate a framework for analyzing and designing agroindustrial projects. It is written primarily for public sector analysts in developing countries, but it should also be useful to private sector managers financing or managing agroindustries. The analytical framework may also be helpful to organizations starting agroindustrial projects in more developed economies. This initial chapter will define agroindustry, introduce the analytical framework, and describe the scope of the book and the organization of the remaining chapters.

Defining Agroindustry

An agroindustry is an enterprise that processes agricultural raw materials, including ground and tree crops as well as livestock.[1] The degree of processing can vary tremendously, ranging from the cleaning and grading of apples to the milling of rice, to the cooking, mixing, and chemical alteration that create a textured vegetable food. As shown in table 1-1, agroindustries can be roughly categorized according to the degree the raw material is transformed. In general, capital investment, technological complexity, and managerial requirements increase in proportion with the degree of transformation. The purposes of transforming raw food and fiber are to create an edible or usable form, to increase storability, to create a more easily transportable form, and to enhance palatability or nutritional value.[2] Agroindustrial projects are unique because of

---

1. Agroindustries are essentially processing operations and thus represent only one component in the larger, seed-to-consumer agribusiness system.
2. The closer one moves to level iv in table 1-1, the more similar the enterprise becomes to nonagroindustrial manufacturing operations.

Table 1-1. *Categories of Agroindustry*
by Level of Transformative Process

I	II	III	IV
Processing activity			
Cleaning	Ginning	Cooking	Chemical alteration
Grading	Milling	Pasteurization	Texturization
	Cutting	Canning	
	Mixing	Dehydration	
		Freezing	
		Weaving	
		Extraction	
		Assembly	
Illustrative products			
Fresh fruits	Cereal grains	Dairy products	Instant foods
Fresh vegetables	Meats	Fruits and vege-	Textured vegetable
Eggs	Spices	tables	products
	Animal feeds	Meats	Tires
	Jute	Sauces	
	Cotton	Textiles and gar-	
	Lumber	ments	
	Rubber	Oils	
		Furniture	
		Sugar	
		Beverages	

three characteristics of their raw materials: seasonality, perishability, and variability.[3] Each of these main characteristics merits brief discussion.

Seasonality

Because raw material for agroindustries is biological, its supply is seasonal, available at the end of the crop or livestock-reproduction cycle. Although raw material supply is usually available only during one or two brief periods during the year, the demand for the finished product is relatively constant throughout the year. Unlike the nonagroindustrial manufacturer, the food- or fiber-process-

---

3. Not all agroindustries share these characteristics equally; for example, timber, unlike tomatoes, does not have a marked, seasonal production pattern, nor is it very perishable.

ing factory must contend with a supply-and-demand imbalance and problems of inventory management, production scheduling, and coordination among the production, processing, and marketing segments of the farm-to-consumer chain.

Perishability

Unlike the raw material used in nonagroindustries, biological raw materials are perishable and often quite fragile. For this reason, agroindustrial products require greater speed and care in handling and storage, which can also affect the nutritional quality of food products by reducing the damage or deterioration of the raw material.

Variability

The final distinctive characteristic of agroindustries is the variability in the quantity and quality of raw materials. Quantity is uncertain because of weather changes or damage to crops or livestock from disease. Quality varies because standardization of raw materials remains elusive, even though there have been advances in animal and plant genetics (this is in sharp contrast to the extensive specifications for standard materials used in other manufacturing industries). These variations exert additional pressure on an agroindustrial plant's production scheduling and quality-control operations.

In addition, two other characteristics should be emphasized, although they are not unique to agroindustries. The raw material in agroindustries is usually the major cost component. Thus, procurement operations fundamentally shape the economics of the enterprises. Many agroindustrial products are also necessities, and governmental interest and involvement in agroindustrial activities consequently will often be high, thereby making social, economic, and political considerations particularly relevant to project analysis.

A Force for Development

Agroindustry contributes significantly to a nation's economic development for four reasons. First, agroindustries are a nation's primary method of transforming raw agricultural products into finished products for consumption. Second, agroindustries often constitute the majority of a developing nation's manufacturing sector. Third, agroindustrial products are frequently the major exports from a developing nation. Fourth, the food system provides the nation with nutrients critical to the well-being of an expanding population. Each of these factors is examined below.

A door for agriculture

Most agricultural products, including subsistence products, are processed to some extent. A nation therefore cannot fully use its agronomic resources without agroindustries. A survey of rice-milling practices in six provinces in Thailand revealed that approximately 95 percent of rice was processed in rice mills rather than hand-milled in the home.[4] Similarly, a survey of 1,687 households in four regions in Guatemala revealed that 98 percent of families took their corn to mills for grinding and subsequently made the corn dough into tortillas in the home.[5] Mechanical processing saves consumer time and effort, and, as economies develop, these savings become more important to consumers. Thus, the demand and necessity for processing services increase as agricultural production increases.

Agroindustries are not merely reactionary; they also generate new demand backward to the farm sector for more or different agricultural output. A processing plant can open new crop opportunities to farmers and, by so doing, create additional farm revenue. In some instances this has permitted subsistence farmers to increase their income by entering the commercial market. In other cases it has enabled new lands or lands unsuitable for traditional crops to be brought under cultivation. In regional development programs, agroindustries have provided the economic justification for rural infrastructure such as penetration roads that provide access to raw materials, electrical installations for plant operation, or irrigation facilities. Agroindustries can also function as an economic focal point for cooperatives for small farmers and related community-development activities.

It is important to note that the process by which rural indus-

4. James E. Austin (ed.), *Global Malnutrition and Cereal Fortification* (Cambridge, Mass.: Ballinger Publishing Co., 1979), p. 244.
5. Ibid., p. 162.

trialization occurs can greatly affect the significance and permanence of the developmental stimulus agroindustries give to rural communities. One critical element appears to be community participation. A United Nations Industrial Development Organization (UNIDO) Expert Group concluded that the "formulation of policies and programmes of rural industrialization had to involve a much greater participation of the people in order to be effective."[6] The group recognized that the rural population's lack of resources and limited absorptive capacity would require special external assistance to enable fuller participation and effectiveness.

When backward linkages occur, they generally increase farm employment. This is significant because agriculture remains the primary employer in developing nations, whereas manufacturing employs less of the labor force. This can be observed in Latin America, where agriculture absorbs 38 percent of the labor force but accounts for only 15 percent of the gross national product (GNP), and where manufacturing absorbs 15 percent of the labor force and accounts for 35 percent of the GNP.[7] The power of agroindustries to use domestic resources is also illustrated in a study of Costa Rica, which found that for every 100 colones sold, agroindustries used 45.6 colones of national raw materials and nonagroindustries used 12 colones.[8]

A cornerstone of the manufacturing sector

The importance of agroindustries in the manufacturing sector of developing countries is often not fully realized. In most countries food and fiber processing constitute the foundation of the nation's industrial base. For example, in Central America agroindustries accounted for 78 percent of Nicaragua's manufacturing sector's output in 1971.[9] In Asia, agroindustries in the Philippines generated over 60 percent of the value added in the manufacturing

6. UNIDO, *Industrialization and Rural Development* (New York, 1978), p. 8; also see Bejsin Behari, *Rural Industrialization in India* (New Delhi: Vikas Publishing House, 1976).

7. Inter-American Development Bank (IDB), Division of Agriculture, "Guide to Preparation of Agroindustrial Projects" (Washington, D.C., April 1974; processed), p. 1.

8. Fernando Caldas, "Consideraciones sobre las agroindustrias en Costa Rica" ["Considerations Regarding Agroindustries in Costa Rica"] (New York: UNIDO, August 1976; processed).

9. Banco Central de Nicaragua, *Informe Annual—1970* (Managua, 1971).

sector between 1960 and 1973.[10] In Ecuador, a country between Nicaragua and the Philippines in population and per capita GNP, the pattern is the same: agroindustries are responsible for 69 percent of the value added in the industrial sector.[11]

Agroindustries are more important to the economies of lower-income countries and decline in importance as the countries further industrialize. The initial stages of industrialization draw on the countries' natural agricultural endowment.[12] Chenery and Hoffman have documented that countries diversify in subsequent stages into nonfood and fiber products, frequently as part of an import-substitution strategy.[13] The shifting pattern is shown in table 1-2 for several countries in Latin America, Asia, and Africa.

Although agroindustries tend to account for a smaller relative share of the manufacturing sector as industrial development proceeds, other important transformations within the agroindustrial sector occur. As shown in table 1-3, the per capita consumption of processed foods and the value added per employee in the developing countries' food and beverage industries appear to increase as incomes rise.

Given that the urban population (who consumed relatively more processed foods) of 990 million in developing countries in 1980 will grow to 2,155 million by the year 2000, one can expect a significant growth in the food-processing industries.[14] The mix of processed foods will change to favor those requiring higher levels of transformation (see table 1-1).

10. Bureau of Census and Statistics, *Annual Survey of Manufacturers* (Manila, 1974).

11. IDB, *Identificación de Prioridades de Inversión en el Sector Agropecuario de Ecuador* ["Identification of Investment Priorities in the Agriculture and Cattle Sector of Ecuador"], Agricultural Development Document no. 14 (Washington, D.C., August 1973).

12. An example is textiles, one of the first agroindustries established in developing countries because it produces a basic good and can take advantage of the lower labor costs as well as the agronomic capabilities. As of 1974, 50 percent of the looms and 48 percent of the spindles were installed in developing countries. International Federation of Cotton and Allied Textile Industries (IFGATI), *International Cotton Industry Statistics*, vol. 17 (1974), pp. 13, 19.

13. Hollis B. Chenery, "Patterns of Industrial Growth," *American Economic Review*, vol. 50 (September 1960), pp. 624–54; Walter D. Hoffman, *The Growth of Industrial Economies* (Manchester: University of Manchester Press, 1958).

14. United Nations, *Urban and Rural Population* (New York, 1970), Table 5, pp. 14–19.

Table 1-2. *Contribution of Agroindustry
to Manufacturing Sectors in Selected Developing Countries*
(percent)

Country	Agroindustry	Nonagroindustry
Latin America		
Brazil		
1949	66.1	33.9
1969	41.6	58.4
Colombia		
1953	79.5	20.5
1967–69	63.1	36.9
Costa Rica		
1960	71.0	29.0
1973	53.0	47.0
Mexico		
1950	58.6	41.4
1967–68	51.1	48.9
Venezuela		
1953	73.5	26.5
1971	51.7	48.3
Asia		
Iran		
1963–64	73.3	26.7
1967–68	65.4	34.6
Malaysia		
1963	64.6	35.4
1968–69	48.6	51.4
Pakistan		
1955	75.1	24.9
1968–70	66.7	33.3
Philippines		
1956	74.5	25.5
1968–70	62.7	37.3
South Korea		
1958	67.9	52.1
1967–69	55.1	44.9
Taiwan		
1954	68.8	31.2
1967–69	43.1	56.3
Thailand		
1954	76.4	23.6
1967–69	65.4	34.6
Turkey		
1950	79.1	20.9
1967–69	53.8	46.2

(*Table continues on the following page.*)

Table 1-2 *(continued)*

Country	Agroindustry	Nonagroindustry
Africa		
Kenya		
1954	60.3	39.7
1967–69	51.7	48.3
Nigeria		
1950	78.2	21.8
1967–68	67.3	32.7

Source: United Nations Industrial Development Organization (UNIDO), *Growth of World Industry*, vol. 2 (New York, 1973), except data on Costa Rica, from Fernando Caldas, "Consideraciones sobre las agroindustrias en Costa Rica" (UNIDO, August 1976; processed).

Table 1-3. *Value Added and Processed Food Sales in Developing Countries, 1975*
(U.S. dollars)

Developing country	Value added per employee in food and beverage industry	Per capita processed food sales	
		Total population	Urban population
Low-income	667	17	53
Middle-income	3,607	48	112
High-income	7,504	158	252

Source: United Nations Centre on Transnational Corporations, "Transnational Corporations in Food and Beverage Processing," unedited version, ST/CTC/19 (New York, 1980), p. 182.

A further indicator of the importance of agroindustries within the manufacturing sector is their employment-generating capacity. In developing countries in 1975, 9,734,000 people were engaged in the food and beverage industries alone; excluding fiber-processing agroindustries, this figure constitutes 18.9 percent of all the jobs in the manufacturing sector.[15] The annual average growth rate in employment in these jobs between 1970 and 1975 was 6.3 per-

15. United Nations Centre on Transnational Corporations, "Transnational Corporations in Food and Beverage Processing," unedited version, ST/CTC/19 (New York, 1980), p. 7.

cent; this far exceeds the population growth rate of 2.8 percent and was particularly important as an employment source in the lowest-income countries, in which the annual average growth rate between 1970 and 1975 in these jobs was 7.9 percent.[16] In this regard the significance of small-scale industries (ssi's) is particularly notable: ssi's generally provide most of the jobs in the manufacturing sector, and most ssi's are agroindustries. For example, ssi's in Indonesia account for approxmiately 75 percent of manufacturing employment even though they contribute only 16 percent of the sector's value added.[17] Thus, improving the viability of small and medium-size agroindustries appears to be especially important to achieving employment objectives. A final point on the employment benefits of agroindustries is that they frequently provide major employment opportunities for women. In India, for example, 25 percent of the workers in the food and beverage industry are women, as are 60 percent in the tobacco industry; in Sri Lanka, women constitute 42 percent of the labor force of the food-and-drink industry; in Cyprus, 36 percent; in Honduras, 21 percent.[18]

Although these figures demonstrate the economic significance of the agroindustrial sector, they understate its effect on a nation's other industries. A large percentage of the commercial sector is engaged in distributing agroindustrial products. Agroindustries similarly contribute to the financial sector and other service industries. Finally, enterprises manufacturing materials for agroindustry, such as agrochemicals and farm machinery, depend on the demand for agricultural produce, and this demand in turn depends on a viable food- and fiber-processing industry.

An export generator

The most important natural resource of most developing countries is agriculture. Agricultural produce has an international demand and, because production capacity frequently exceeds local

16. Ibid.
17. Donald R. Snodgrass, "Small-scale Manufacturing Industries: Patterns, Trends, and Possible Policies," Development Discussion Paper no. 54 (Cambridge, Mass.: Harvard University, Institute for International Development, March 1979), pp. 12–13.
18. UNIDO, *Industrialization and Rural Development*, pp. 39–44.

consumption, there is an opportunity for export. A nation must process the raw material, however, into a form suitable for export. Even minimal processing, such as drying grain or ginning cotton, adds economic value to the produce and generates foreign exchange. The value added in agroindustrial products tends to exceed that of other manufactured exports because other exports frequently rely on imported components, and export agroindustries tend over time to increase the domestic percentage of value added by increasing the degree of raw material processing. For example, ginning operations are extended to textile weaving and apparel manufacturing; beef carcasses are processed into portion cuts or canned products; coffee beans are transformed into instant and freeze-dried coffee. Such incremental industrialization not only increases value added but also creates products that are further differentiated, have higher income elasticities, and are more insulated from the price fluctuations of less processed commodities.[19]

The dominant export function of agroindustrial manufacturers is evident from the export statistics of developing countries. In the case of Nicaragua, cited above, over 85 percent of exports between 1960 and 1970 were agroindustrial products.[20] Closer scrutiny reveals another export pattern—heavy reliance on a few principal products. In 1970 cotton, coffee, and meat products constituted 57 percent of Nicaragua's total exports. In general, the narrower the product line, the more exposed the nation is to the dramatic fluctuations of international commodity prices and, thus, the greater is the country's external dependence.

Yet the Nicaraguan statistics also reveal the benefits of a diversified export portfolio. In 1960 cotton products accounted for 27 percent of total exports; by 1965 the "white gold" had boomed to 51 percent, but five years later it had decreased by 50 percent. During the same ten-year period, processed beef exports rose from $3 million (5 percent of exports) to $27 million (15 percent of exports), thereby largely offsetting the decline in cotton exports.[21]

---

19. Increased transformation will not necessarily improve price stability. Some intermediate products—for example, palm oil—may face markets as unstable as those for less processed commodities, whereas the investment—and hence the capital exposure—in intermediate products has increased. Value added has increased but the price risk has not necessarily decreased.

20. Central Bank of Nicaragua, *Informe Anual—1970* (Managua, 1971).

21. All dollar figures in this study are in U.S. dollars.

By broadening its agroindustrial export portfolio, a country may be able to obtain countercyclical price insurance.

The potential macro-level benefits accruing to a nation through its exports should be further scrutinized at the micro-level to ascertain how different groups share in these benefits. Nicaragua under the ruling Somoza family was an instructive example of how agro-industries can increase the concentration of wealth and exacerbate income inequities. The Nicaraguan Government of National Reconstruction (Gobierno de Reconstrucción Nacional), which supplanted the Somoza regime, is presently attempting to operate these same agroindustrial assets, now expropriated, so as to eliminate the longstanding inequities.

The nutrition dimension

It has been estimated that over one billion people in developing countries are undernourished.[22] By generating income to low-income farmers and providing employment to low-income workers, agroindustries can improve a population's diet and, if agroindustries stimulate increased food production for the domestic economy, they can furnish a country with a better chance to survive the Malthusian food-population race. Furthermore, the food-processing industry is important to the nutritional well-being of the urban poor because of their dependence on commercial food channels. Agroindustrial projects can, however, have adverse nutritional consequences if they are not carefully designed, and projects must be closely examined to prevent the undesirable nutritional effects they may cause. For example, an agroindustry might cause farmers to shift from staples, thus lowering the supply and raising the price. The income from a cash crop may or may not be large enough to improve family diets. In any case, the nutrition of low-income, landless workers or urban consumers may suffer from such a rise in the price of staples. Alternatively, higher prices in the international market can lead to an increase in the export of staples and a decrease in the domestic supply. Finally, some forms of processing can decrease a food product's nutritional value.

22. Shlomo Reutlinger and Marcelo Selowsky, *Malnutrition and Poverty: Magnitude and Policy Options*, World Bank Staff Occasional Papers, no. 23 (Baltimore: Johns Hopkins University Press, 1976). "Billion" is equivalent to "thousand million."

Growing importance of agroindustry

The importance of agroindustries in a nation's development is being increasingly recognized, and financing for agroindustrial projects has grown significantly in recent years. By 1973 the World Bank, the Inter-American Development Bank (IDB), and the United States Agency for International Development (USAID) had funded fifty-eight projects, with a total of $384 million, in Latin America and the Caribbean. All of these agencies have subsequently increased their funding and are giving particular emphasis to SSI's and rural industrialization. In fiscal year 1980 the World Bank alone approved thirty-nine loans totaling $1.8 billion to twenty-seven countries for financing projects that, at least in part, included agroindustries. As of June 30, 1976, the International Finance Corporation (IFC) had invested $42.7 million in food-processing operations.[23]

Several countries (Mexico among them) have made agroindustries a cornerstone in their development plans. The growing importance of agroindustries as development tools increases the demands on, and responsibilities of, project analysts. The following section sets forth a framework through which analysts can meet this challenge.

An Analytical Framework

The essence of effective project analysis is the systematic application of analytical techniques tailored to fit a project's characteristics. Agroindustrial projects are often evaluated as either agricultural or manufacturing projects, a division that reflects the fragmented structure of the analyzing institutions themselves: ministries are split into agriculture and industry; development banks are specialized as agricultural or industrial; and analysts are categorized as agricultural economists or industrial engineers. But agroindustrial projects are by nature *inter*sectoral, and a framework for the sectoral analysis of agroindustrial projects is inappropriate for two reasons. First, the nature of the raw material distinguishes

23. John W. Lowe, "The IFC and the Agribusiness Sector," *Finance and Development*, vol. 14, no. 1 (March 1977), p. 25.

agroindustries from industries that are not subject to the pressures and vicissitudes of agronomic forces. Second, processing differentiates agroindustrial projects from agricultural projects that focus primarily on production. Agriculture and industry must be seen as being integrated if an appropriate framework for agroindustrial project analysis is to be developed.

Systems analysis

In this book is presented a framework for project analysis that is constructed around agroindustries' unique characteristics and that is capable of incorporating analyses of the financial and socioeconomic dimensions within which agroindustries lie. It treats agroindustries as a component in a larger, seed-to-consumer system of related parts, in which the system linkages create an interdependence between the actions and actors in the system. This method necessarily examines the project implications of interdependent stages of the system. These implications hold whether the agroindustry is a state-owned enterprise or a privately owned organization.

Agribusiness has been defined as involving those individuals and institutions engaged in the production, processing, transport, storage, financing, marketing, and regulation of the world's food and fiber products.[24] The agribusiness system is composed of operators, supporters, and coordinators. The operating organizations are the farmers, transporters, warehousers, processors, and distributors who handle the physical commodity as it flows from the farm to the marketplace. The supporting institutions are the farm suppliers, financial entities, and research centers that contribute to the system's operators. The coordinators are governments, contractors, futures markets, and industrial associations that integrate the various stages of the food-and-fiber system. These major components of the food-and-fiber system are illustrated in figure 1.

The focus of this book is on the processing segment of the agroindustrial system. Although this may appear to be a narrower

---

24. The term "agribusiness" was coined by John H. Davis and Ray A. Goldberg, who subsequently elaborated their concept in the book *A Concept of Agribusiness* (Boston: Harvard University, Graduate School of Business Administration, Division of Research, 1967).

Figure 1. *Flow Chart for Agroindustry*

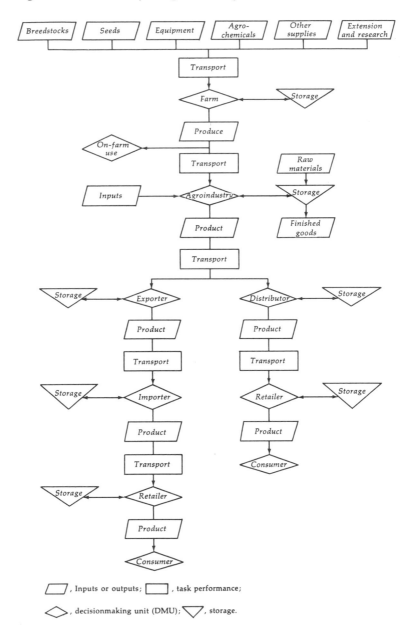

, Inputs or outputs; ⬜ , task performance;

◇ , decisionmaking unit (DMU); ▽ , storage.

focus than indicated by the definition of agribusiness given above, it is necessary to maintain a broad, systems perspective for agro-industrial project analysis. Because agroindustries are the center of the agricultural chain, it is essential to examine both the farm—the source of raw material supply—and the market—the outlet for the processed products. In effect, systems analysis aids the overall design and implementation of agroindustrial projects by examining three operating activities of an agroindustry: marketing, procurement, and processing.

Before the discussion proceeds, the importance of systems analysis can be illustrated by a situation reported to the author by an official of a West African government. The government had adopted an industrial development strategy aimed at maximizing the value added of the nation's agroindustrial products. The country had been exporting cottonseed for many years; hence, the government accepted a proposal for a cottonseed-oil extracting plant because it was consistent with the value-added development strategy.

The plant was constructed, but the minimum capacity of the equipment required more cottonseed than was available, necessitating a program to increase cotton production. The subsequent production program included land redistribution, farm reorganization, and extensive technical assistance, and the increased plantings stimulated the construction of a textile mill. Cotton production did increase greatly, but apparently the risks of planting cotton were too great or the benefits too low: the farmers continued to plant subsistence crops to which they gave harvest priority. This created a labor shortage for picking the cotton, and large amounts had to be left in the fields. As a result, the oil plant and textile mill operated below capacity. The textile mill was forced to import cotton yarn from Pakistan to meet its need for raw material. In addition, more cottonseed oil was produced than the local cooking-oil refinery could process, thereby necessitating the export of the unrefined oil. Similarly, the nation lacked a domestic market for the cottonseed meal because the animal-feed and livestock industries were not at a stage of development capable of absorbing this by-product. An important protein source had to be channeled into the international market at low prices, while at the same time costly animal protein products were being imported.

This example reveals the disadvantages of a narrow view of agroindustrial projects. The project illustrated was seen as one value-adding processing operation rather than as a part of a multi-stage, multiproduct commodity system. The failure to recognize the interdependencies in that system created shortages of the raw material and excesses of the processed products. Analysts must view agroindustries as part of a larger milieu and recognize that the viability of such projects depends on the success of the whole multidimensional system.

Three components of the analytical framework

Agroindustrial systems analysis focuses on project design as it relates to the marketing, procurement, and processing activities. It is equally important, however, to apply the techniques of financial and economic analysis to assess the financial viability and social costs and benefits of a project. Thus, the analytical framework for agroindustrial project analysis contains three components, comprises systems, financial, and economic analyses. This book will focus on the first of these components by further examining the agroindustrial marketing, procurement, and processing activities. These activities have financial and economic implications and thereby inevitably relate the systems analysis to the financial and economic. Because an abundant literature on financial and economic analysis and methodology is available, these subjects will not be examined in detail in the text. Instead, a list of readings on financial and economic analytical techniques may be found in the first section of the bibliography. Yet the importance of these components of agroindustrial project analysis merits brief discussion.

Owners and investors in agroindustrial enterprises are concerned about their return on investment. It is therefore essential to conduct a financial analysis to compute these returns. Unless such computations prove the project financially viable, private investors will channel their funds elsewhere. If the agroindustry is to be a state-owned enterprise, negative financial returns would suggest a subsidy. An adequate financial return on investment, however, is not sufficient reason to launch a project. Society's return on the resources it devotes to the project must also be determined. This requires an economic analysis, which will provide public policy-makers with a means of ranking projects according to their social costs and benefits, an assessment necessary if the use of scarce capital resources to meet the country's development objectives is to be maximized. Managers in the private sector should similarly be interested in cost-benefit analysis to evaluate the developmental significance of their efforts.[25]

Financial and economic assessments share some analytical techniques, such as cash-flow computation and present value discounting, but the two methods do differ. Financial analysis employs market prices for inputs, whereas economic analysis uses "shadow" prices to reflect the opportunity costs of those inputs to society. Similarly, financial analysis considers certain items such as costs of taxes, but economic analysis considers these as transfer payments from one segment of society to another and therefore excludes them from the analysis. The same is true for subsidies: under financial analysis they are revenue, but under economic analysis they are a transfer payment. Because of these differences, the economic streams for the same project can yield significantly different results from the two analyses.

The differences do not imply, however, that one method takes precedence over the other. A project that is highly profitable to the entrepreneur but yields minimal benefits to society is not likely to win the approval of a concerned public policymaker. Similarly, a project that has a high socioeconomic return but produces only small profits for the entrepreneur is not likely to find any private investors. Thus, if private capital is needed, it is necessary to examine both the financial and economic returns and select projects that meet both criteria or to redesign them so that they do. The framework for agroindustrial analysis—comprising systems, financial, and economic analyses—should be viewed as one package. Yet even the application of this analytical package to a project will not produce an automatic investment decision: many projects demand other considerations—for example, political or social priorities. Project analysis merely provides one basis for decisionmakers to investigate the interaction of the social and economic factors implicit in agroindustrial investments.

The Scope of the Book

Agroindustrial projects have four stages: identification, analysis and design, implementation, and evaluation. In keeping with its

25. Louis Wells, Jr., "Social Cost-Benefit Analysis for MNC's [Multinational Corporations]," *Harvard Business Review*, vol. 53, no. 2 (March-April, 1975), pp. 40–47.

emphasis on systems analysis and the processing segment of agro-industry, this book focuses on the second, perhaps most critical yet least-studied, stage. Obviously, the analyst should not neglect the other stages, and they will be briefly discussed in this section. The scope of the book is limited in another way: it focuses on the analysis of individual agroindustrial projects. The orientation is toward the micro level, but it is important for the analyst to recognize that the viability of specific projects can be significantly affected by macro-level policies. Although it is beyond the scope of this presentation to discuss these macro-level policies extensively, this section will briefly indicate the policy areas particularly relevant to agroindustrial projects.

Project cycle

The cycle of an agroindustrial project is composed of the four stages mentioned above, each of which will be examined in turn.

IDENTIFICATION. The analyst's first task is to identify potential projects and select the most promising. During this phase, development agencies or banks should encourage and solicit project proposals.

To assess the proposals, project analysts should develop a set of criteria based on the agroindustrial areas that are weak or present new opportunities. Such areas can be identified by studies of the commodity system that examine industrial subsectors. It is worthwhile to collect information on the structure, volume, flow, and financial and economic performance of commodity systems because additional agroindustrial investments can improve the efficiency or growth of these systems.[26] A commodity-system data bank can help avoid undesirable investments or highlight areas

26. Ray A. Goldberg, *Agribusiness Coordination* (Boston: Harvard University, Graduate School of Business Administration, 1968); Charles Slater and others, *Market Processes in La Paz, Bolivia*, Report no. 3 (East Lansing: Michigan State University, 1969); Harold Riley and others, *Market Coordination in the Development of the Canca Valley Region, Colombia*, Report no. 5 (East Lansing: Michigan State University, 1970); James E. Austin, *Marketing Adjustments to Production Modernization* (Managua: Instituto Centroamericano de Administración de Empresas, 1972); and Ray A. Goldberg, *Agribusiness Management for Developing Countries in Latin America* (Cambridge, Mass.: Ballinger Publishing Co., 1976).

that warrant further attention. In addition, information on the commodity system would lower the costs preceding the feasibility study for those commodity projects because the data are common to all project analyses, making it practicable to examine small projects. The subsector profiles provide the development planner with the information to consider a strategy for all sectors.

Marketing studies of an industry can also be viewed as a capital investment in information. Such studies could assess volume, prices, standards, and competition on domestic and export markets for selected products that are judged to have high market potential because of existing market needs or emerging demand trends. Although studies of this kind are often too costly for individual project proponents, they are more feasible when conducted for multiple projects.

PROJECT ANALYSIS AND DESIGN. Project proposals that survive the initial screening must be examined more closely for their operational, financial, economic, and social feasibility and desirability. The analyst should attempt to redesign the project to overcome weaknesses in the proposal. This will be discussed in subsequent chapters.

IMPLEMENTATION. The leap from proposal on paper to project operation is often a long and precarious one. The task of the analyst is to increase the probability of a successful transit by paying adequate attention to critical managerial factors during the project appraisal. The focus of this study's analytical framework on the marketing, procurement, and processing activities of an agroindustrial project attempts to clarify these managerial factors.

EVALUATION. Once a project has begun, a project analyst is responsible for monitoring its progress to locate and remedy deviations from projected performance. Such evaluation should follow indicators of financial and economic performance. Poor performance is caused by problems in the original project design, changes in the external environment, or weaknesses in operations management. The supervising analyst should identify the causes of the substandard performance, determine to what extent they can be controlled, and suggest corrective measures. This evaluation is vital to the streamlining of a project's design and its ultimate success.

When possible, the analyst who evaluated the project design

should remain with the project throughout implementation to provide continuity from design through evaluation. The analyst's familiarity with the project should improve the monitoring and redesign of the project.

Considerations at the macro level

Although this book concentrates on the analysis of individual agroindustrial projects, single projects cannot be divorced from the larger context of development policy. Macro-level policies likely to affect agroindustries are briefly discussed in the remainder of this section.

INTERNATIONAL TRADE. In the case of exports, fiscal incentives such as tax rebates, or monetary incentives such as preferential foreign exchange rates, have been used to provide an added stimulus to attract capital and managerial resources to agroindustrial projects. Care must be exercised, however, that fiscal incentives do not favor substitution of labor by capital, unless the former is in scarce supply. In any event, tax incentives do not appear to be critical factors in the investment decisions of most entrepreneurs.[27] In the case of imports, policy incentives have included tariff and quota exemptions for essential inputs, such as packaging or raw materials, that are not locally available. Although providing access to vital inputs may help establish an agroindustry, this and like measures should generally coincide with efforts to develop local input production. Only then will the full developmental benefits of the linkage characteristics of agroindustry be realized.

REGIONAL DEVELOPMENT. Agroindustries can play a critical role in regional development because of their relationship to agricultural production and urban marketing. Fiscal incentives and investments in public sector infrastructure can attract industry to new regions. For example, penetration roads can allow a processing plant to procure raw materials and thereby develop the region's agricultural resources more fully. Policies may have different effects on enter-

27. The policymaker should weigh whether the proposed measures will create greater price distortions that would disfavor agriculture; a move toward market-oriented scarcity pricing might create a more effective incentive.

prises of different size, and policymakers should attempt to ascertain these.[28]

RESEARCH. Another policy area related to resource development and project viability is research. It is difficult for private industry to do genetic research and field experimentation, yet the continued supply of raw materials depends on agronomic research, and the lack of such information can be a severe deterrent to instituting a new project. Government-sponsored research programs, in conjunction with industry, can create the production information vital to project development. For outputs, governments should support market research because it is frequently industry related and too costly for a single firm to conduct. For example, governments could investigate marketing needs through commodity sectoral studies.

QUALITY CONTROL. Quality control is particularly important to export-oriented agroindustries. Because these industries can generate foreign exchange, governments and the industries should ensure that the export product is of a high quality by setting standards and instituting inspection systems. Quality control is also important domestically, in the monitoring of the safety and nutritional value of processed foods.

INCOMES POLICIES. Incomes policies can include support prices to farmers or price controls on finished consumer goods. Both measures affect an agroindustrial processing plant—the former by affecting raw material costs and the latter by limiting the price of processed goods. Thus, governments can significantly affect project profitability.

MONETARY POLICY. Monetary policy can determine interest rates and credit availability for certain projects and can therefore mobilize resources to agroindustries of different kinds, sizes, and locations. Inflation will also influence project economics.

NATIONAL PLANNING. The feasibility of an agroindustry can be significantly influenced by its relationship to overall national de-

28. For example, it may be necessary to use quite different policy instruments to affect different-size ssr's. See Snodgrass, "Small-scale Manufacturing," pp. 12–13.

velopment plans. For example, the government's rural development or trade strategies and policies could directly impinge on project viability. The role a government wishes foreign investors to play in its national development strategy can also be significant for agroindustries. Transnational corporations have considerable investments in agroindustrial operations in developing countries. For example, approximately one-fourth of the foreign investments of food and beverage companies in the more developed nations are in the developing countries, and these corporations account for one-eighth of the output of the developing countries' food processing industries.[29] In the larger and more affluent markets—such as Mexico, Brazil, Argentina, and Venezuela—the transnationals account for over one-fourth of the local industries.

Organization of the Chapters

The systems method of analysis is applied in chapters 2, 3, and 4 to the three main areas of agroindustrial activity. The *marketing factor* is investigated in chapter 2, and the issues of consumer preference, market segmentation, demand forecasting, product pricing, distribution channels, and competitive forces are addressed. The *procurement factor* is discussed in chapter 3, and the relations between the production and processing stages and methods of managing the flow of raw material from the farm to the factory are examined. A discussion of the *processing factor* and the related issues of technology selection, plant location, inventory management, processing inputs, and operational considerations follows in chapter 4.

Although each of these chapters explores a particular operational activity of agroindustries, systems analysis presupposes an underlying recognition of the close interdependence of agricultural operations. Consequently, each separate analysis considers one activity's effect on the remaining two. The systems method implies

29. United Nations Centre on Transnational Corporations, "Transnational Corporations," pp. 17, 20; also see chapter 4 of the report for a discussion of government policies toward transnational corporations operating in the food industry.

an interactive process whereby the effect of one decision can be traced through the whole system to reveal consequences that, at times, necessitate modifying the original project design.

Each chapter identifies problem areas common to agroindustrial projects. To guide the analyst in performing project analysis, central issues are reduced to question form within each chapter, and these lists are compiled in full in appendix B. The questions indicate the information needed to thoroughly analyze each particular activity. All the relevant data are seldom available to the analyst, however, and the cost of collecting data relative to the size of the project or capabilities of the personnel may not be justified. Thus, not all questions can or need be answered to carry out effective project analysis. Project decisions are always made with imperfect information; nevertheless, it is crucial for the analyst to recognize what information is desirable so that data gaps can be recognized and, if not remedied through new data collection, overcome by explicit assumptions. It is better to know what questions have gone unanswered than never to have asked—risks can be better judged this way.

The goal of this book is to provide agroindustrial project analysts with practical guidelines from actual experience and to distill theoretical concepts and translate them into a form useful to practitioners. Examples of actual agroindustrial projects have been included but, given the diverse characteristics of each project, no analytical framework can be detailed enough to encompass every project. Because a framework is ultimately only a guide, the analyst must adapt its analytical concepts to the specific project's peculiarities. The critical judgment required of project analysts in using the framework for analysis presented here is intended to heighten their decision orientation when examining projects and thus to minimize the effort spent on the marginal aspects of projects. Many of the examples given are from ongoing agroindustries rather than proposed enterprises. It is useful for project analysts to be familiar with problems that mature enterprises encounter so that they may anticipate operational difficulties in a proposed project's design.

Because of its position in the food system, an agroindustry affects the nutritional status of a nation's population. Malnutrition has caused massive human suffering and the severe erosion of human capital in many countries. Although a viable food-and-fiber system is fundamental to dealing with the problem of malnutrition, project analysts have paid little attention to the nutritional aspect of agro-industries. Consequently, each chapter will raise nutritional issues for analysts to consider.[30]

Agroindustrial analysts are generally economists, agronomists, industrial engineers, or management specialists. The material of this book is presented in a manner that is compatible with these diverse aspects of agroindustries; the framework provided is broad and can be used by different professionals. Some information may be common knowledge to certain disciplines but new to others, and each user should adapt the framework to his or her field of expertise and the particulars of the project being studied. Again, this adaptation will enrich the analytical process, strengthen the framework, and consequently increase the viability of the agroindustrial project. A selected bibliography on various topics related to the financial and economic components of the analysis and to the marketing, procurement, and processing activities is included for those readers wishing to obtain more detailed information on the particular analytical techniques and concepts discussed in the chapters, as well as an appendix (appendix A) in which indicative costs of various food-processing technologies are compiled.

30. For a more detailed analysis of issues involved in the design of nutrition programs, see James E. Austin, *Confronting Urban Malnutrition: The Design of Nutrition Programs*, World Bank Staff Occasional Papers, no. 28 (Baltimore: Johns Hopkins University Press, 1980), and James E. Austin and Marian Zeitlin (eds.), *Nutrition Intervention in Developing Countries: An Overview of Nutrition Programs*, U.S. Agency for International Development (USAID) (Cambridge, Mass.: Oelgeschlager, Gunn, and Hain, 1980).

2

The Marketing Factor

THE VIABILITY OF AN AGROINDUSTRIAL PROJECT requires soundness in each of the project's three basic component activities—procurement, processing, and marketing. Although this is the operational sequence of the components from the standpoint of the external environment, the marketing factor is the logical starting point for project analysis: unless there is adequate demand for a project, it has no economic basis.

Primary Elements

A marketing analysis examines the external environment's response to a firm's product by analyzing consumer characteristics and the competition. Such information helps the firm to design procurement and processing strategies and construct a comprehensive marketing plan. This process is illustrated in figure 2.

A prerequisite as valid as market demand is the agronomic capacity to grow the raw material upon which the agroindustry will depend. The agroindustrial system obviously requires both markets and supplies for project success. A production bias, however, has historically dominated agricultural and agroindustrial project analysis, and markets were considered secondary issues. Yet Say's Law is not always reliable; supply does not necessarily create its own demand.[1] Too often projects have failed because of a mismatch of production and marketing.[2] Because agronomic feasibility

1. Benjamin Higgins, *Economic Development* (New York: W. W. Norton, 1968), p. 68.
2. A community-run small-scale industry (SSI) in Mexico became very successful only after it reviewed consumers' needs and eliminated several products that had been produced only because the production skills existed; United Nations Industrial Development Organization (UNIDO), "Case Study on the People's Collective Industries of Jalisco," in *Industrialization and Rural Development* (New York, 1978), p. 28.

Figure 2. Agroindustrial Marketing Analysis

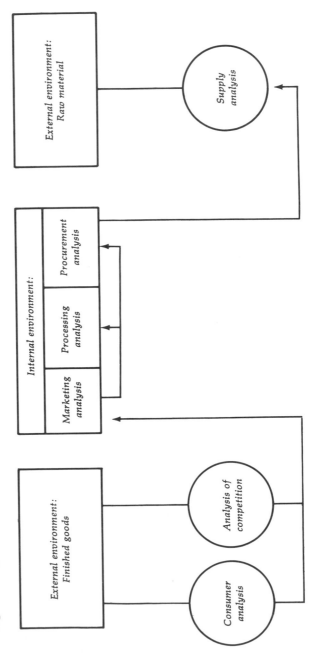

testing consumes significant time and resources (such as land, inputs, research), it is economical to identify market needs first. In addition, land has multiple crop or livestock usages, and market information can help an analyst choose among such alternatives. Furthermore, a market analysis can identify a product need that is agronomically feasible but has not been considered. For example, based on a study of export market needs, the producers in one Central American country began growing okra, even though it had never been produced there and was not locally consumed.

As indicated in chapter 1, agroindustrial products differ from other products in the unique characteristics of their raw materials (perishability, seasonality, and variability in quantity and quality) and in their frequent status as necessities. The marketing of agroindustrial products will consequently differ from the marketing of nonagroindustrial goods, and their necessity will often attract political attention to, and government control of, prices, quality, and distribution.

The primary elements that will be considered in the marketing analysis of an agroindustrial project are the following:

- *Consumer analysis.* The analyst examines consumer needs, market segmentation, the purchasing process, and market research.
- *Analysis of the competitive environment.* The analyst examines market structure, basis of competition, and institutional constraints.
- *The marketing plan.* The analyst defines the elements of product design, pricing, distribution, and promotion that constitute the firm's marketing strategy.
- *Demand forecasting.* The analyst examines techniques and considerations for projecting sales.

Consumer Analysis

To define the project's potential consumer, the analyst must identify the needs the product will satisfy, the market segments the product will serve, and the method of purchase. Market research is needed to obtain this information. If the agroindustrial product is a common one, the amount of new consumer analysis needed may be minimal. A new product, however, will require a thorough analysis.

Consumer needs

The purpose of marketing is to define and meet consumer needs. Socially responsible marketing does not create needs but responds to needs existing within a cultural context.

Consumer needs are created by a complex interaction of physiological, sociological, and psychological motives. For processed foods, which constitute the bulk of agroindustrial products, consumer needs are frequently expressed as preferences for a product's taste, smell, color, texture, and appearance. More fundamentally, the needs relate to nutritional requirements and appetite satisfaction. For fiber products such as cotton, jute, or wood, consumers are industrial buyers (often from another agroindustry) whose main interests are price and quality.

Another motive affecting consumer purchasing is social status. For example, the Yucatán region of southern Mexico has a plant called *chaya* that grows wild and is rich in protein. It was eaten by the ancient Maya along with maize and beans in a nutritionally sound diet. Over the years, *chaya* became known as a "poor man's" food, and it was consumed less and less, even though the people's diet was short of protein. Consumer preferences also depend on several needs in addition to intrinsic product qualities, including such usage conveniences as packaging or cooking ease. To develop an appropriate product and an effective marketing program, an analyst should examine consumers' motives for purchasing a product.

Market segmentation

To match a product with the needs of consumers, it is necessary to divide consumers into groups or market segments. There are numerous variables that categorize consumers and define segments—for example, geographic location. In a country as large as India, there are considerable differences in language and culture among states, and an agroindustry attempting to market its products nationally would have to adjust its communication and the product to these differences.[3] Geographic location often reveals ethnic or regional taste differences: consumers in northern Thailand prefer glutinous rice, whereas consumers in central and southern regions prefer nonglutinous varieties. Age and sex of consumers are two other common segmenting variables—for example, weaning foods for infants or protein- and calorie-rich foods for pregnant or lactating women. Another differentiating variable is income level because effective demand and food preferences change as income levels rise. This variable clearly affects product pricing and can easily affect other product characteristics. Market-research data from a study to determine the feasibility of marketing nutritionally fortified cookies and crackers in a Central American country is presented in table 2-1. These data are stratified by income level and indicate the size of the package most frequently bought. The table reveals a difference between the high- and low-income consumers: the low-income purchasers prefer smaller packages, probably because these consumers have reduced incomes and cash flow. In order to service the nation's large, low-income market segment, the product's packaging would have to be adjusted according to this analysis by the income-level variable. Another market differentiation is between domestic and export consumers— export consumers frequently demand higher product quality than do domestic consumers.

In addition to being selected by socioeconomic or demographic characteristics, market segments can also be defined by their needs. For example, products can be viewed as necessities, status items, or convenience goods, and this definition will influence their pricing, promotion, and distribution. A final segmenting method is by user—for instance, industrial (bakeries, for example), institutional (for example, restaurants), wholesale or retail, or end-consumer.

Market segmentation is used to identify potential consumers because an appropriate marketing strategy cannot be determined until the market has been defined. The consumer groups can be sequenced into subsegments according to various descriptive characteristics, as in figure 3, or organized into matrixes, as in figure 4.

3. ssi's based in rural areas should first assess local needs and ascertain whether the rural market might be sufficient without having to tie into urban markets. Meeting local needs might increase the regional development effect of the agroindustry.

Table 2-1. *Preferred Form and Size of Packaging for Cookies and Crackers in Guatemala*
(percentage of purchasers polled)

Package form and size	Income of purchaser		
	Low	Medium	High
Can			
Small	5	9	5
Medium	12	27	20
Large	15	25	36
Total preference	32	61	61
Box			
Small	7	8	4
Medium	6	6	4
Large	9	8	13
Total preference	22	22	21
Other small package			
Total preference	34	10	14
No preference			
Total preference	12	7	4

Source: MARPLAN (Guatemala City, 1972).

Figure 3. *Illustrative Subsegmentation Process*

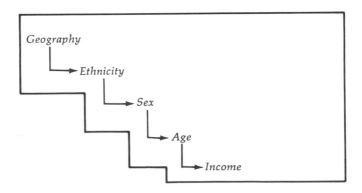

Figure 4. *Illustrative Segmentation Matrixes*

Income

	A	B	C	D
20–29				
30–39				
40–49				
50+				

Age

Income and sex

		A		B		C		D	
		M	F	M	F	M	F	M	F
South	I								
	M								
West	I								
	M								
North	I								
	M								

Region and ethnicity[a]

a. I, Indian; M, mestizo.

Because market segmentation limits the agroindustrial project's options, the analyst should select a segment based on the competitive environment and the strengths and weaknesses of the company. Once the analyst has selected a segment, he or she can use the consumer characteristics to develop the marketing plan.

Because of the characteristics of the raw material, agroindustrial projects have many product-processing options. When deciding on the degree of processing, the project analyst must consider the marketing consequences. One West African nation, seeking to increase the value added in its exports, decided to make cocoa butter rather than export the beans whole. The market segment for cocoa butter, however, was smaller than the segment for whole beans and more susceptible to erosion by substitute products, and butter was charged higher tariffs than were beans. As a result, the nation had an unprofitable and underutilized plant.

The buying process

Understanding the buying process can guide the project analyst in designing the marketing plan. The buying process can be examined by looking at *who* decides to purchase the product, *how* they decide, and *when* and *where* they make the purchase.

The *who* is often more than one person. It is important for the project analyst to identify all the individuals constituting the decisionmaking unit (DMU) to know where to direct promotion. Individual members (for example, parent and child) of the DMU might be reached by different methods. Because the end consumer is often not the buyer, the processor is more interested in the buyer than the consumer. For example, infants consume baby food, but parents purchase it. Baby-food manufacturers therefore choose flavors based on parents' preferences.

Consumers make purchasing decisions in a variety of ways. *How* they make these decisions influences a marketing plan's promotion, pricing, and distribution. Low-price items are often purchased on impulse; hence, product display and packaging are determining factors. Expensive items are frequently planned purchases that, because of the cash outlay, require greater information for the consumer. For planned purchases, such as major items of clothing, brand image and sales advice are significant factors.

When people buy involves frequency and seasonality. Staple products such as rice are bought frequently, whereas luxury products are purchased occasionally. Purchasing frequency affects several marketing issues, pricing among them. A manufacturer, for example, can sell rice at a low price because it is purchased frequently, but a product such as palm hearts requires a high price to offset its low volume. The demand for some agroindustrial products, such as ice cream and hot breakfast foods, is seasonal. This poses additional questions for inventory management, cash flow, and diversification of product line, questions that will be examined further in chapter 4.

Where people purchase varies by segment and product. High-income consumers tend to use supermarkets or specialty stores, whereas low-income consumers shop at small, neighborhood stores or public markets. Although buyers are willing to travel for planned purchases, they buy impulse items according to what is available. When designing a distribution system, manufacturers should consider where consumer segments shop. For example, the Mexican government's food-marketing agency, Compañía Nacional de Subsistencias Populares (CONASUPO), situated its low-price food stores in low-income neighborhoods to reach these consumers.

Market research

Market research attempts to identify consumer needs, market segments, and the buying process to facilitate sound marketing decisions. The process consists of four steps: data specification, source identification, data collection, and data analysis (see the second section of the bibliography for further reference).

DATA SPECIFICATION. The private or public marketer must define his or her market information needs. These needs will vary according to the type of agroindustrial project, the marketer's familiarity with the product's market, and the financial risks.[4]

SOURCE IDENTIFICATION. After identifying the necessary information, a marketer should locate the information's primary and sec-

---

4. Definition of the "market" and the "consumer" is also essential for social interventions such as governmental programs to serve malnourished children. For the information requirements relevant to such undertakings, see James E. Austin, *Confronting Urban Malnutrition: The Design of Nutrition Programs*, World Bank Staff Occasional Papers, no. 28 (Baltimore: Johns Hopkins University Press, 1980), pp. 18–51.

ondary sources. Primary sources include the product's consumers, producers, distributors, and field experts. Secondary sources—such as government feasibility reports, industrial publications, loan analyses, census data, and international agency studies—can also be useful.

DATA COLLECTION. Data can be collected formally or informally. Formal data collection techniques consist of an explicit research design, a statistical sampling, and standardized information-collection procedures such as telephone, mail, or direct interview surveys.[5] Informal collection methods can include talking to a few consumers or distributors or examining company data or competing products. Sometimes marketers conduct controlled experiments to test such aspects of a marketing plan as price or promotion. Econometric modeling—which will be discussed later in the chapter— is a research tool used to forecast demand. The financial and managerial resources of agroindustrial ssi's are often too limited to conduct thorough market research, and this function may have to be carried out through government assistance to the entire industry or sector.

DATA ANALYSIS. Data analysis requires interpretation of the information to fit specific informational needs—for example, the testing of product concepts, characteristics, pricing, or promotion. Before making the final analysis, however, marketers and project analysts should verify all sources and collection methods because the quality of the findings depends on the reliability of the data.

The value of market research information should be weighed against its cost so that the researcher will collect an adequate amount of quality data at the least cost. Such data should enable better decisions, which will in turn generate economic benefits in excess of the cost of the data collection and analysis. Locating the point of least cost and maximum benefit requires judgment. The decisionmaker must assess the probable effects on sales or costs of more market research and compare these effects against the incremental data costs. Perfect information is never possible, and

5. Direct surveys and interviews appear most feasible in developing nations, given the sometimes limited coverage and other deficiencies of postal and telephone services.

decisionmaking is always done under uncertainty. Market research is intended to reduce this uncertainty at a reasonable cost.

For example, the manager of a vegetable-oil plant was considering switching from a plastic can to a polyethylene bag for a shortening product because of the cost savings, estimated at $0.01 a container or $10,000 a year for a million-unit output. The marketing director proposed spending $5,000 for a consumer survey and a panel to test the new packaging concept. The manager was not enthusiastic about spending one-half of a year's savings on market research, but he was uncertain about how the new packaging would affect sales. He suspected that there was only a 50 percent chance that sales would fall by more than 10 percent, but the marketing director pointed out that, with the profit margin of $0.10 a unit, a 10 percent drop from 100,000 units would negate the cost savings. He thought that market data would provide the manager with information by which the manager could estimate the effect of the change in packaging. The research was conducted and indicated that one-third of the consumers would not buy the product in the new package because, when they used all the shortening, they recycled the plastic containers to other uses. As a result, the manager estimated, with 90 percent certainty, that sales would drop by 25 percent and generate a loss of $22,500 (1,000,000 units × 25 percent sales loss × 90 percent certainty × $0.10 margin), which would negate the cost savings of the new packaging and result in a net loss.

Salient points for project analysis

A project analyst should consider the following questions when reviewing the consumer and marketing dimensions of an agroindustrial project.

Who are the potential consumers?
- Socioeconomic, cultural, demographic characteristics?
- Market segments?
- Positioning options for the product?

Why would they buy the product?
- Physiological, sociological, psychological needs?
- Expressed reasons for purchasing? sustenance? sensory appeal? status? convenience? necessity?

- Relative importance of needs and reasons?
- Implications for the marketing plan?

How would they buy the product?
- Decisionmaking unit (DMU)?
- Impulse or planned purchase?
- Purchase frequency?
- Seasonality?
- Purchase location?
- Credit to distributors?
- Implications for the marketing plan?

What market information and methods of data collection are needed?
- Data needs?
- Data sources?
- Methods of data collection?
- Reliability?
- Cost?
- Value of additional information?
- Capacity of SSI's to gather?

Analysis of the Competitive Environment

Agroindustrial projects do not exist in a vacuum. They enter a marketplace crowded with agroindustrial firms and products, and their success partly depends on their ability to compete with other firms. Accordingly, a marketing analysis should examine the structure of the market, the basis of competition, and the institutional constraints affecting the competitive environment.

Market structure

Market structure has been a traditional focal point for economists studying industrial organizations and the competitive environment. The structure of a particular market is also relevant to a new firm considering entering it (see "Market structure" in the second section of the bibliography for further reading).

A structural examination of a market can begin by identification of the competitors, which can be public or private enterprises, regional, national, or multinational companies, old or new or branded or unbranded products. The likelihood and significance of new entrants (future competition) in the market must also be assessed, and analysts should consider competition from substitute products (for example, synthetics for cotton, or soft drinks for fruit juices) as well. Products should be identified with their broad industrial classifications: the textile mill is in the fiber business instead of the cotton business, and the juice processor is in the beverage business instead of the fruit juice business. The interdependent nature of agroindustries implies that they must further broaden the concept of competition. Suppliers of raw material who can integrate forward to process their own product are potential competitors—a dairy farm, for instance, could add a processing plant for its milk. Similarly, large buyers may integrate backward to produce a product they use—a supermarket chain, for instance, might construct a vegetable cannery.

A structural analysis should also identify the number of competitors to determine the oligopolistic tendencies in the market. The location of other firms' markets and raw materials also carries implications for competition. Finally, the size of competing firms in net worth (assets), sales volume, and market shares should be examined. Market share is an indication of industrial concentration and suggests the market power of the firms. Data across years is useful for revealing competitive trends in the market.

Documenting market structure is analogous to the process of market segmentation described previously, which dealt with positioning the product relative to consumer groups. The goal here is to lay out the various competing segments so as to identify the options for positioning the product at a competitive advantage. To understand those options more fully, it is necessary to examine the basis upon which firms compete.

Basis of competition

Competition occurs simultaneously along several parameters. In a perfectly competitive society, price is the primary method of competing. Market imperfections, such as oligopolistic structures, make perfect competition purely theoretical. Nonetheless, that price is an important competitive tool is indicated by consumers' sensitivity to price and the prevalence in the market of price discounting.

Product quality is a second parameter of competition. Price and

quality theoretically yield consumer value, and consumer preference increases in proportion to the value. But, because quality is
subjective, market segments can evaluate quality differently. Sometimes price alone is presumed to indicate quality, and a low price
will create consumer resistance because the price is perceived negatively. It is important to recognize the difference between the intrinsic and perceived quality of a product: brand and image creation
is a strategy of quality competition, whereas packaging and product content are means of quality differentiation.

Service is a third parameter of competition. For agroindustrial
products, service is directed to the distributor or retailer rather than
the end consumer. Fast delivery, inventory supply, promotional
information, and credit and discounts (indirect forms of price competition)—all are services calculated to obtain product support.
Such service is particularly relevant for industrial buyers, where
supply uncertainty is high, or when outlet coverage and shelf display space are critical.

New products go through a product life cycle (PLC) during which
their market experience changes. (Although this pattern is worth
noting, it is less applicable to food products than to other manufactured items.) A model of the PLC is presented in figure 5.[6] When
a new product enters the marketplace, there are few competitors,
and the product's newness insulates it from price competition. As
the product's success grows, it attracts competition that stimulates
primary demand, expands the entire market, and may also introduce price competition. As the product matures and differences
among brands decrease, the basis of competition shifts more to
price. Improvements in the production processes or economies of
scale lead to reductions in production cost that allow more aggressive price cutting. The product, perhaps modified or promoted differently, may extend the maturity stage, but its sales eventually
decline because the market is satiated or captured by new products.
Some commodities, such as cereal grains, avoid the final decline
because they are necessities. As incomes rise, however, consumers

6. The PLC model has been used to explain domestic and international trade
flows and competitive patterns. For an excellent overview of the international
application of the model, see Louis T. Wells, Jr. (ed.), *The Product Life Cycle
and International Trade* (Boston: Harvard University, Graduate School of
Business Administration, Division of Research, 1972).

Figure 5. *Product Life Cycle* (PLC)

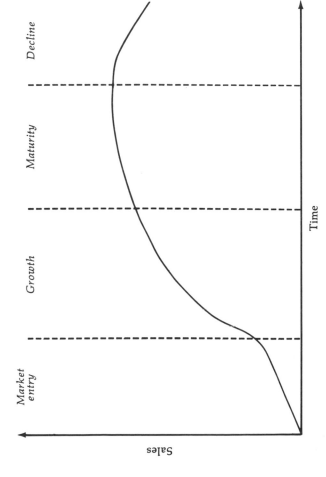

prefer further processed forms of the staple. Manufacturers benefit by identifying the stage of the PLC at which their product will enter.

The market environment and project feasibility are also affected by barriers to entry in the industry; a discussion of the four most common of these follows.

ECONOMIES OF SCALE IN PROCESSING. A capital-intensive processing enterprise with significant economies of scale has a lower cost structure for an ongoing producer with a large share of the market than for a new, low-volume company. A new company in this market would have difficulty competing with the price of a developed company's product. In addition, the limited purchasing power in developing countries lessens the effective demand and limits the viability of small manufacturers. Excess capacity is another entry deterrent in agroindustries. Finally, given the scarcity of capital in developing countries, capital requirements may impede entrants.

ABSOLUTE COST DISADVANTAGE. A firm may possess a patented or proprietary formula or production technique that creates a lower cost structure regardless of the scale of its operation. An example is a manufacturer of dehydrated potatoes, whose manufacturing process can only be approximated by a newcomer through extensive research and development.

VERTICAL SYSTEM CONTROL. In agroindustry, barriers to market entry can arise because firms integrate vertically to control the raw material inputs or the distribution channels. This can prohibit new operations or put them at an absolute cost disadvantage. An example of vertical control is the Central American banana plantations that control packing and marketing operations.

BRAND FRANCHISE. Existing products may have strong consumer loyalty. In this case, a new company must price its product significantly lower than the original product or advertise heavily to attract consumers from their usual brand. Similarly, imported or foreign brands frequently enjoy higher prestige and thus create a barrier to local producers.

The project analyst should weigh the entry barriers because an otherwise attractive project may not be viable if the barriers to entering a market are severe. Public policymakers may wish to take actions to remove these barriers.

Institutional constraints

The competitive environment is also influenced by constraints from economic, health, political, and legal institutions. Tariffs, import quotas, sanitary standards, export incentives, price controls, subsidies, licensing, antitrust statutes, and patent requirements— all are within these categories.

Tariffs are commonly used economic constraints. These international duties can act as competitive barriers to the agroindustry's penetration of export markets or, conversely, can shield a domestic market from import competition. The level and longevity of tariffs should be evaluated in terms of their effects on the proposed product's competitive position. Some possible ramifications are indicated by the following case. A flour mill in a Southeast Asian nation was established during a time of high import duties. Because of the tariff, the firm had a large market share and high profits and grew complacent in its attitude toward its marketing operation. When the government subsequently reduced the import tariff, the company was unable to compete effectively with imported flour because its marketing system had never been well developed. Import quotas also control the competitive environment, and, finally, export promotion incentives are often used to increase the exporters' ability to compete in the foreign market.

Sanitary standards administered by governmental health or agricultural agencies are a further constraint to competition. For example, countries in which aftosa (foot-and-mouth disease) is endemic are not permitted to export fresh meat to the United States— Argentine beef exporters, for instance, cannot compete in this market unless their beef is cooked.

Examples of politically motivated economic constraints are price controls and subsidies. Because many food products are necessities, they become a political concern and are subject to price regulation. In effect, this regulation eliminates price as a competitive factor and can lower the product's profit margin as raw material and processing costs increase but the price for finished goods is constrained by the government. Governments may subsidize both private and state-owned processors to offset these losses. In some countries (India, Pakistan, and Mexico, for instance), the government operates retail outlets to provide necessities to consumers at subsidized prices. This practice tends to affect the private sector outlets by also regulating their prices. If the food-marketing system of the private sector is not functioning in a way that permits attainment of a country's social goals, then the government will, and should, intervene. In fully centrally planned economies, the state obviously assumes the price-formulating function of the marketplace. In most developing countries, however, a mixed economy exists. Industrial licensing is another form of government regulation that affects entry and operation.

Legal constraints such as antitrust legislation are enacted to ensure that industrial behavior is consistent with perceived national goals. In countries with small markets, cartels are encouraged. Patents on processing techniques or equipment can also affect agroindustrial competition. Although patents are presumed to stimulate innovation, they are also barriers to market entry. Knowledge of these various economic, political, and legal constraints will heighten the analyst's understanding of the competitive market.

Salient points for project analysis

The analyst should consider the following questions when examining the competitive dimension of the market.

What is the product's market structure?
- Existing competitors?
- Role of substitutes?
- How many competitors?
- Location relative to markets and raw material?
- Size of sales, assets, market share?
- Changes in market shares?

What is the basis of competition in the industry?
- Consumer price sensitivity?
- Prevalence of price discounting?
- Consumer sensitivity to quality?
- Importance of branding?
- Special services to distributors?
- Stage of product life cycle (PLC)?
- Extent of entry barriers from economies of scale? absolute costs? vertical system control? brand franchise? capital requirements?

How do institutional constraints affect the competitive environment?
- Economic constraints? tariffs? quotas?
- Health constraints? sanitary standards?
- Political constraints? price controls? subsidies? industrial licensing? direct government intervention?
- Legal constraints? antitrust legislation? patents?

The Marketing Plan

The data from the analyses of the consumer and the competitive environment are the basis for a project's marketing plan. The purpose of the plan is to position the firm's product most advantageously in relation to its consumers and competition. The elements of the plan are product design, pricing, promotion, and distribution. These constitute the company's "marketing mix," the core of the marketing strategy.

Product design

Most products have several design options. Even staples such as rice can assume various forms (for example, enriched, parboiled, long or short grain) and packaging (for example, cardboard box, polyethylene or cloth bag). Among the design considerations for agroindustrial products are taste, texture, cooking ease, color, odor, form, nutritive value, convenience, size, and packaging.[7] These characteristics should be matched with consumers' expectations of quality and usage yet kept within the market segment's price range. Costly product improvements must therefore be weighed against the product's resultant price.

The product should be designed by the project's marketing and production personnel because marketing identifies the needs for production's designs, including prototypes that production can make for field testing. When the final design adjustments have been made, full-scale production and marketing begins (see figure 6).

---

7. For fiber, leather, or wood agroindustrial products, factors such as durability, malleability, washability, and fashion should be considered.

Figure 6. *Product Design Process*

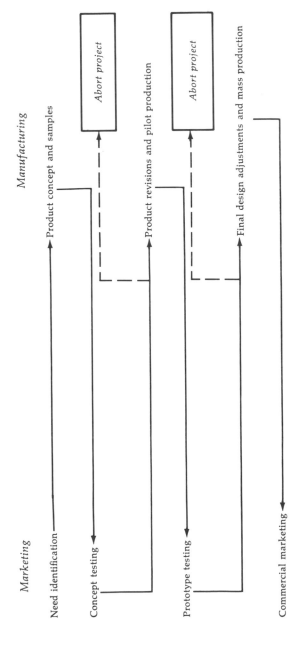

Marketing   *Manufacturing*

Need identification ──────────→ Product concept and samples

Concept testing ──────────────→ Abort project

Product revisions and pilot production

Prototype testing ────────────→ Abort project

Final design adjustments and mass production

Commercial marketing

ssi's may need governmental assistance to design the initial product. Market research should continue throughout the life of the product so that the product's design can be modified to fit consumers' changing needs.

Analysts should recognize that consumers' preferences are not always in the consumers' interests. For example, polished white rice is treated with talc and glucose because consumers prefer white rice with luster. But the talc and glucose coating must be washed away prior to consumption, a process that depletes the rice of vitamin B. Moreover, talc contains asbestos, which may be carcinogenic if ingested in sufficient quantities. For nutritional and economic reasons, the preference for treated white rice should be discouraged.

Pricing

A firm should choose its pricing strategy according to its competitive environment and market segment. The following pricing strategies are the most common.

COST-PLUS PRICING. In cost-plus pricing, the firm adds a margin to its costs for nonmanufacturing costs and profit. For example, if a pair of shoes cost $6 to produce and sells for $10, the markup is 40 percent ([selling price — costs] ÷ selling price). As a percentage of costs, the markup is 66⅔ percent ([selling price ÷ cost] — cost).[8] A more refined approach is to calculate a markup that will generate a selected return on investment at an expected sales volume. The cost-plus strategy is feasible when there is little or no competition—for example, in regulated utilities or food staples, whose prices are determined by the government.

PENETRATION PRICING. Penetration pricing is the setting of prices at levels lower than the competition's in order to enter an existing market. Pricing is used to overcome barriers to market entry or to reach a market segment that would be excluded at higher prices. This strategy is intended to capture a larger market share and establish a firm market position.

---

8. The markup on a cost basis may be derived from the markup on the price basis as follows: price-basis markup ÷ [100 percent — price-basis markup].

PREDATORY OR PREEMPTIVE PRICING. Predatory pricing is an aggressive approach that underprices existing competitors to erode their market position severely. Preemptive pricing underprices the product to prevent new firms from entering the market. This latter strategy, although it creates only a temporary entry barrier, is equally aggressive. These pricing methods can exert excessive market power that may require public regulation.

LOSS-LEADER PRICING. The loss-leader strategy prices one product below cost to attract consumers in the hope that they will purchase other products in a company's line.

SKIMMING. In contrast to the previous strategies, skimming sets high prices to attract or "skim off" the price-insensitive segment of the market. This method is often possible early in the PLC, when differentiation is high and competition low, or when duties are high or imports prohibited.

PRICE LEADERSHIP. With price leadership, the prevailing price is determined by one firm and followed by others. Coordination among sellers often exists without a formal cartel organization in oligopolies marketing undifferentiated products. In this case there is a high risk of market shares' changing with price changes. Tacit collusion in price leadership is usually subject to public monitoring.

ADMINISTERED PRICES. Prices are administered in regulated industries or industries with cartels. The successful efforts of the Organization of Petroleum-Exporting Countries (OPEC) cartel to increase oil prices have led to attempts to organize agroindustrial cartels for products such as bananas and sugar. These attempts have failed because of the large number of producers, the less essential nature of the products, and the existence of substitute products.

CONTROLLED OR SUBSIDIZED PRICES. Because many food products are staples, governments often institute price controls, thus eliminating managements' influence over the price variable. When the commodity is also exported, there may be dual prices, with the international price exceeding the domestic. This may cause the firm to divert production into the international market, which may lead the government to impose a domestic quota system. For example, in one Latin American country with price controls and quotas, sugar processors resisted efforts to fortify sugar with vitamin A because the government would then more closely inspect the flows of production. Alternatively, governments operate stores that sell staple rations at subsidized prices to low-income consumers. Examples of these government controls are ration shops in Pakistan, "fair price shops" in India, and food stamp programs in Colombia and Mexico.

MARKET PRICES. The forces of supply and demand in the market set prices for most agroindustrial commodities. Predictably, most developing countries are pricetakers, and leading export countries are pricemakers. For example, the price of rice in Bangkok—or wheat or corn on the Chicago Board of Trade—serve as reference points for the industry. There are multiple prices, however, to account for the numerous grades, shipment points, and destinations of agroindustrial products. To reduce some of the uncertainty of market-price variability, some firms have initiated contracts either fixed or tied to futures-market prices.[9]

A firm's pricing strategy should be flexible enough to be able to meet changing market conditions. One response is for a firm to move down the price curve first by skimming, and then by gradually reducing the price to expand the market, thus achieving economies of scale and meeting the competition of new firms.

Promotion

Almost all products are promoted to some extent in that consumers are provided with product information (price, quality, and so on) to use in the buying decision. Even a superior product will not reach its sales potential unless consumers are aware of its advantages. The promotional needs of staples and international commodities are less than those of other products, but they still exist. The primary tasks in formulating the promotional strategy are deciding whom to reach, what to say, and how to say it.

AUDIENCE. The consumer analysis identifies the DMU that is the target of the firm's promotion and specifies differences among members of the DMU (for example, parent, child, sex, age). But because the end consumer is not always the decisionmaker, firms

9. This procedure was used, for example, by one of the leading Japanese trading firms in contracting for corn from Thailand. See "C. Itoh and Co., Ltd.," Case Study 4-576-041 (Boston: Harvard University, Graduate School of Business Administration, September 1975).

must often design promotion for both the purchaser and the end consumer.

Promotion directed toward the end user is a critical component in a "pull" strategy to stimulate consumer demand so that end users will demand that retailers offer the product, thereby generating a backward demand and pulling the product from the producer through the distributors to the consumers. Promotion can also be directed at wholesale and retail distributors in a "push" strategy by which the firm attempts to convince distributors of the product's advantages so that they will move the product through to the consumer.

Promotional strategies should be designed to avoid adversely affecting low-income groups. Some researchers have asserted that advertising directed toward marginal consumers creates a negative incentive to save and thus diverts scarce resources from needed productive investments to consumption goods.[10] The influence of a firm's promotion on a country's economic development depends on factors such as those suggested by Nielsen: wealth of audiences, degree of commercial differentiation in products, extent of primary versus secondary demand, and luxury nature of the goods.[11]

Promotion of food products should also be designed to avoid adverse nutritional consequences. The analyst should assess the effect of increased product consumption on the nutritional well-being of the low-income groups. If the product can displace others, the analyst should estimate the relative costs to consumers in caloric or protein content if nutritional intake might be decreased. Infant formulas, which have replaced breastfeeding in some developing countries (even though breast milk is cheaper, of superior nutritional value, and more sanitary), exemplify the adverse nutritional effects a new product can have.[12] Media advertising and other sales techniques were among the factors that led many low-income women—through appeals to convenience and status

---

10. See the second section of the bibliography for selected readings on this issue.

11. Richard P. Nielsen, "Marketing and Development in LDC's," *Columbia Journal of World Business*, vol. 9, no. 4 (Winter 1974), pp. 46–49.

12. Alan Berg, *The Nutrition Factor* (Washington, D.C.: The Brookings Institution, 1973), pp. 89–106. The author estimates that the lost economic value of reduced breastfeeding in developing countries is in the range of hundreds of millions of dollars.

consciousness—to view bottle feeding as a superior method of nourishing infants. The high price of the product relative to the low incomes led some of these consumers to dilute the formula to make it stretch further, thus greatly reducing its nutritional value. Furthermore, because of the low level of education and the lack of potable water, hygienic cooking facilities, and adequate fuel in poor communities, sometimes the formula was mixed with unpotable water. The environmental constraints created a high probability of product misuse. The consequences have been fatal for some infants. Firms should avoid stimulating excessive demand through promotion when a product is nutritionally unsound for consumers or when there is a high probability of product misuse.

MESSAGE. The promotional message should be derived from an evaluation of consumer informational needs and the analysis of the competitive market. Because consumer informational needs vary, there may be numerous promotional objectives, including supplying factual product information, generating product awareness, creating product image, stimulating immediate purchase, and providing reinforcement after purchase.

Some promotion is intended simply to stimulate primary demand for a category of products, especially when the product is new or there is little other advertising. Branding is used to stimulate selective demand for a particular company's product and is more effective when the product can be physically differentiated from those of competitors. It is often difficult for agroindustries to differentiate their products, particularly when the processing is minor. Nevertheless, agroindustries have achieved product differentiation by instituting rigorous quality-control programs. Libyan groundnuts at one point had prices 25 percent above the prevailing world market price because of such control methods. Bananas and Colombian coffee have been branded with similar success. Branding, however, places a significant responsibility on quality control at the processing and procurement stages because poor quality in a branded product can greatly hurt its image and future sales. Finally, promotional messages should be designed to meet the audience's capacity to understand and follow instructions on usage.

VEHICLE. Promotional messages can be communicated to audiences by direct or indirect methods. Direct methods are face-to-face encounters or telephone selling through salespeople. These are generally more costly and have a lower breadth and coverage than indirect methods but a stronger effect on consumer behavior.[13]

Indirect promotional vehicles include television, radio, film, newspapers, periodicals, billboards, posters, and leaflets. The distinctions among them reflect differences in the characteristics of the target audience. For example, if the audience has a low literacy rate, a firm would choose oral rather than written media. Likewise, lower-income segments would not be reached by television advertising but might be reached by transistor radios. Mass media vehicles can cover broad audiences at frequent intervals.

Direct and indirect techniques of promotion are not mutually exclusive—if it is cost beneficial to use both techniques, they can be mutually reinforcing. In general, if the product is new, complex, expensive, and not easily differentiated, the consumer buying process is complicated and risky, and personal selling is more effective. Both techniques can be used with push or pull strategies.

Distribution

Distribution is important in the marketing mix because it links the processor to the marketplace. It should be examined by looking at the structure and functions of the distribution system to assess integration and outlet options.

STRUCTURE. The structure of the distribution system can be described by the length of its channels—that is, the number of intermediaries between the manufacturer and the consumer. It can also be described by the breadth of the system—the number of wholesalers and retailers at each level. Finally, it can be described by the nature of the institutions operating it. At the wholesale level, these institutions can be full-line, limited-line, or specialty wholesalers who buy and resell goods. Agents and brokers also operate as wholesalers, but as commissioned sales agents for the manufacturer rather than as buyers of merchandise. Government marketing boards can also be wholesalers, particularly for major export products. Retail stores can be categorized according to the kind of goods offered—for example, convenience, shopping, or specialty.

---

13. Telephone contact can achieve broad coverage and high frequency even compared with some mass methods—for example, mailings or advertising in periodicals. In many developing countries, however, telephone ownership is limited and service defective, thereby diminishing this method's applicability.

FUNCTIONS. Many functions must be performed to move the product from the processor to the consumer—including logistical operations (transport, assembly, repackaging, storage, and inventory management), financing, promotion, and information collection. These intermediary functions and services must be performed regardless of whether the system is free market or centrally planned. SSI's may be able to realize considerable economies if they organize marketing associations to perform these functions collectively. Some additional functions and actors are involved when marketing is for export.[14]

OPPORTUNITIES FOR INTEGRATION. A processor must decide between using the distribution services of the existing institutions and undertaking distribution itself. To develop independent distribution services, a firm must integrate forward. This requires a cost-benefit analysis of existing and projected operations as well as an evaluation of storage and handling facilities and the distributor's service dependability.

Transport is a major factor when the product is perishable. For example, a Central American exporter of fresh vegetables had a transport network from farm to packing plant by pickup truck, plant to port by refrigerated trailer truck, port to port by ferry, port to distributor by trailer truck, and distributor to retailer by truck and train. With such complex networks, it is often difficult to obtain the necessary vehicles, transport services, or managerial logistics, and in a project's early stages these deficiencies can create serious and costly bottlenecks. In Central America's early attempts to export to the U.S. market, transport service was uncoordinated and, at times, represented one-third of total costs (see table 2-2). In Turkey, a ferry system was developed to bypass the land route to Europe because slow overland transport had hampered exports of fresh produce.

Many governments have modernized wholesaling facilities for fresh produce such as fruit, vegetables, grains, and meat. This can be a highly desirable investment because it reduces waste, preserves product quality (including nutrients), shortens the length of the distribution channel, and increases transport and handling efficiencies. The success of modern facilities depends, however, on

14. See "Export marketing" in the second section of the bibliography for references on this subject.

Table 2-2. *Cost Structure of Selected Central American Exported Fresh Produce, 1971–72*
(U.S. dollars per box exported)

	Exported produce					
	Cucumbers (Guatemala)		Melons			
			El Salvador		Honduras	
Cost item	Export cost	Per- centage of total	Export cost	Per- centage of total	Export cost	Per- centage of total
Production	1.29	16.6	1.96	31.8	3.52	41.3
Packing	1.41	18.1	1.20	19.5	1.10	12.9
Transport	1.67	21.5	1.96	31.8	2.87	33.6
Tariffs	1.42	18.3	0.45	7.3	0.55	6.5
Handling and repacking	1.18	15.1	n.a.	n.a.	0.25	2.9
Commissions	0.81	10.4	0.59	9.6	0.24	2.8
Total	7.78	100.0	6.16	100.0	8.53	100.0

n.a., Not available.
Source: James E. Austin, direct survey; cited in Ray A. Goldberg, *Agribusiness Management for Developing Countries—Latin America* (Cambridge, Mass.: Ballinger Publishing Co., 1974), p. 180.

ensuring the patronage of buyers and sellers. One new wholesale market in an Asian nation had difficulties getting wholesalers to use the facility because it was located on the outskirts of the city and was difficult for the wholesalers' retail customers to reach, although it was easily accessible to producers and processors supplying the wholesalers. Furthermore, people were forbidden to sleep overnight in the new facilities, a proscription that conflicted with social traditions.

A further motive for analyzing the distribution system's structure and functions is to locate the system's controlling force. The locus of power is often indicated by structural concentration—for example, a few processors who supply many distributors or many processors who supply a few distributors (a large supermarket chain, for instance). When structural concentration occurs, the power lies with the few because many organizations are dependent on them. Power may also be derived by controlling a central function such as storage or transport. If the distribution system's power is highly concentrated and the risk to the processor is high, the processor should consider forward integration. With increased control, however, there are also greater capital and managerial resource requirements. In addition, the relatively fixed investment in distribution facilities may decrease the firm's flexibility in responding to the new distribution requirements of a changing market.

Integration can be precluded if the government has introduced a marketing board as a monopsonistic wholesaler. Marketing boards serve numerous functions, including the provision of technical assistance, promotion of products or plans, quality control, price stabilization, and the provision of infrastructure.[15]

Forward vertical integration is also difficult because of the strength of distributor-retailer relations. This can be illustrated by the Southeast Asian flour mill described in the previous section (under "Institutional constraints") that had neglected its marketing system when protected by an import tariff. When the tariff was removed, the company had no sales force and relied entirely on wholesalers who gave preference to imported brands. The mill considered organizing a sales force and selling directly to the bakeries, but the bakeries resisted because they had developed loyalties to the distributors. The wholesalers gave credit to the bakers (often to meet personal needs), had long-standing friendships, and sometimes were even related by family ties. These social bonds created barriers to forward vertical integration.

OUTLET OPTIONS. If the analyst decides to use existing distribution channels, he or she must then choose wholesalers and retailers. As discussed above, wholesalers can be selected according to cost, quality, dependability, and control. Retail outlets, however, must reflect the product, the market segment, and the prospective consumers' buying process. This decision is necessary even when processors vertically integrate through the wholesaling level.

The retail options are intensive, selective, or exclusive, and they differ in breadth. The intensive strategy maximizes breadth and consumer coverage and is appropriate for low-priced, undifferentiated, high-use products such as sugar. Because consumers will not shop around for these products, coverage is critical to intensive retailing. The selective strategy employs a few chosen stores and is appropriate for expensive and differentiated products that people will selectively shop for and that can be sold through direct personal selling—for example, a suit of clothes. With exclusive distribution, one outlet is given the franchise for the product within a competitive area. This is appropriate for specialty goods that are either highly complex, costly items or luxury, low-use items such as caviar.

In all cases, the analyst should review the proposed distribution system to ensure an appropriate product-distribution fit.

Integrating the mix

The elements of the marketing mix should be designed to be internally consistent and mutually reinforcing. For example, it would not be consistent to have an extensive distribution system with a skimming price strategy, or an exclusive distribution system with a broad, mass media promotional program.

The marketing mix for a particular product must also relate to the company's entire line so that sales will not be diverted from another of the company's products. If sales are diverted, such "cannibalization" can make an individual product appear highly successful without significantly benefiting the company as a whole. Sometimes the marketing mix can be adjusted so that consumers will remain with the company and "trade up" from one product to a higher-price, more elaborate product—for example, from canned peas to frozen mixed vegetables. The marketing approach must also be related to a company's financial, organizational, production, and procurement operations.

The integration of the marketing components into an internally consistent whole that is compatible with the company's product line and the other managerial functions constitutes the marketing plan.[16] Based on the enterprise's marketing objectives, it should guide the project through the competitive market environment.

16. See Philip Kotler, *Marketing Decision Making: A Model-building Approach* (New York: Holt, Rinehart & Winston, 1971) and *Marketing Management: Analysis, Planning and Control*, 3d ed. (Englewood Cliffs, N.J.: Prentice-Hall, 1976).

Responses by the competition to the marketing plan will vary according to the product's market position. For example, there will be little reaction when the product is patented, when it captures a low market share, when it is not comparable to competing products, when it is only modestly profitable, or when competitors are financially weak.

Even ssi's should have explicit marketing plans, which will be relatively simple because of the narrow product lines and small scale but which will serve as a check to ensure attention to the necessary marketing activities. More often than not, it is marketing problems that cause ssi's to fail or stagnate.

Salient points for project analysis

The marketing plan should be an integral part of all project proposals. In reviewing it, a project analyst should consider the following questions.

Was the product adequately designed?
- Characteristics desired by consumers?
- Price of quality improvements?
- Product's concept and prototype tested?
- Results and design adjustments?
- Final product market tested?
- Design fit with consumer needs?
- Capacity of ssi's to design?

Was the appropriate pricing strategy adopted?
- Cost-plus pricing feasible?
- Prices regulated? subsidized?
- Basis for markup?
- Penetration pricing's effect on entry barriers, market size and share?
- Legal or ethical acceptability of predatory or preemptive pricing?
- Volume effect of loss-leader pricing?
- Feasibility of skimming?
- Industry price leader?
- Effects of following or deviating from price leader?
- Basis of administered prices?
- Futures markets or long-term contracts as pricing mechanism?
- Expected changes in strategy over time?

Was the right promotional strategy formulated?
- Audience identified?
- Consumers' information needs specified?
- Information supplied by competitors?
- Purpose of message?
- Impact of branding?
- Adequacy of quality-control procedures?
- Form of communication consistent with audience's capacity to receive?
- Chance of misinterpretation or misuse?
- Share of audience reached?
- Frequency of reach?
- Cost of promotional vehicle?
- Cost effectiveness of combined direct and indirect promotional techniques?

Will the distribution system effectively link the manufacturer to the marketplace?
- Length of channels?
- Number of distributors at each level?
- Types of wholesalers and retailers?
- Logistical functions performed?
- Service functions performed?
- Economies to small-scale industries (ssi's) by joint marketing?
- Cost, quality, and dependability of existing services and facilities?
- Distributor's managerial capabilities and customer orientation?
- Locus and basis of controlling power in channel?
- Effect of power distribution on project viability?
- Control, economic, and managerial implications of forward vertical integration?
- Social, political, or legal barriers to forward integration?
- Intensive, selective, or exclusive retail-outlet strategy?
- Consistency of outlet intensity with market segment and buying process?

Are elements of the marketing mix integrated in a viable marketing plan?
- Elements of mix internally consistent?
- Effect on other products in company's line?
- Compatibility with company's financial, organizational, production, and procurement operations?

- Likely competitive reaction?
- Adjustments in marketing strategy?

Demand Forecasting

Demand forecasts are needed to estimate the economic implications of the marketing plan and are used to project profitability, financial and raw material needs, and plant capacity. Although final demand projections are dependent on a final marketing plan because it sets the parameters of the market segment, the demand forecasts and marketing plans must be developed simultaneously. For example, the expected market size should be estimated early and compared with the minimum economical size for the plant or with the availability of raw material. If market demand does not support this production scale or exceeds raw material supply, the study need go no further. Similarly, the firm would benefit in selecting elements of the marketing mix by projecting the effect of each at various sales volumes.

Forecasting involves collecting and analyzing past data to understand future market behavior and to reduce the uncertainty of decisionmaking. The analyst should examine the forecasting data and techniques carefully. A discussion of data requirements and forecasting methods, which can be placed in three main categories —judgmental estimates, time-series analyses, and causal models— follows.

Data considerations

Before using data for forecasting, an analyst should consider the kind of data he or she needs—including sources, reliability, and underlying assumptions.

TYPE OF DATA. Forecasts should be made in physical and monetary values, and units of measure should be standardized to facilitate comparisons. Wholesale, retail, and international (free-on-board [f.o.b.], or cost-insurance-freight [c.i.f.]) price data, however, should not be mixed. Distribution markups represent these price level differences. Manufacturer-level prices are the most relevant for agroindustrial demand projections.

Analysts also must decide what time period the data should encompass. This decision usually depends on how representative the prior years have been in relation to the projected period and on which years have used consistent methods of data collection.

Data are most useful when they can be disaggregated to correspond to product categories and market-segment characteristics. This disaggregation is usually not published, and analysts may have to calculate it themselves.

DATA SOURCES. Market sales data can be gathered from primary or secondary sources. Primary sources include reports by trade associations, research studies by educational institutions and international agencies, and company analyses. Data collection from primary sources requires market-research techniques described earlier in the "Consumer Analysis" section of this chapter. Secondary sources include government documents (such as customs statistics, national income-accounts data, industry studies, family budget surveys, or census data) and private sector studies.

DATA RELIABILITY. Analysts should verify the accuracy of the data to ensure reliable projections by reviewing the data-collection techniques, and they should retain a skeptical attitude toward published statistics because erroneous statistics tend to perpetuate themselves. For example, one country's production of wheat flour was estimated in 1960 from a nonrandom sample of wheat mills. The 1970 statistics were still based on the 1960 data, although increased by a factor for the annual population growth. Analysts should be suspicious of historical data that increases uniformly because agroindustries have a significant factor of variability.

In reviewing the data for reliability, analysts should make sure that the data sample was representative and that no historical aberrations occurred. This can be a difficult process. For example, in table 2-3 the historical data for the consumption of tinned milk in Ghana is shown in support of the country's consideration of a tinned milk factory project. An inspection of the statistics might indicate that 1961 was a nonrepresentative year. Further investigation, however, reveals that 1962 and 1963 were actually the nonrepresentative years because the government then had imposed foreign exchange controls and import restrictions. In developing countries, statistics on "apparent consumption" do not necessarily reflect true demand because expenditures can be hindered by import restrictions or other government regulations such as industrial licensing.

Table 2-3. *Tinned Milk Consumption*
in Ghana, 1955–63

Year	Total consumption (containers)	Per capita consumption (fluid ounces)[a]
1955	67,949	20.81
1956	76,549	22.63
1957	95,015	27.37
1958	104,126	29.23
1959	124,968	34.17
1960	131,130	34.93
1961	176,920	45.93
1962	162,676	41.16
1963	168,945	41.67

Source: Economic Development Institute (EDI), *Tinned Milk Market Fore-cast*, EDI Case Study and Exercise Series no. IE-5218-5 (Washington, D.C.: World Bank, June 1976; revised September 1979; processed), p. 7.
a. One fluid ounce = 29.573 milliliters.

DATA ASSUMPTIONS. The preceding example also reveals the importance of examining the underlying assumptions of projections. It is useful to test both the quantity and price assumptions of projections. For example, a prospective spice manufacturer projected sales on the assumption that historical industrial trends would continue (see table 2-4). If prices *or* volume were 10 percent lower than expected, however, profits would fall by 25 percent. If prices *and* volume were 10 percent under forecast, profits (and return on investment) would drop by 47.5 percent. Changes in price or vol-

Table 2-4. *Illustrative Sensitivity Analysis for Spice Sales*
(U.S. dollars)

Sales item	Sales condition		
	Historical trend holds	Prices or volume fall 10 percent	Prices and volume fall 10 percent
Unit price	0.05	0.45	0.45
Total volume	10,000,000	10,000,000	9,000,000
Total revenue	500,000	450,000	405,000
Costs	300,000	300,000	300,000
Profits	200,000	150,000	105,000
Change in profits (percent)	0	25	47.5

ume are magnified when translated into profit. Accordingly, this prospective manufacturer should reevaluate sales assumptions because of their extensive financial consequences.

Forecasting methods

The characteristics, uses, and limitations of the three principal forecasting methods—judgmental estimates, time-series analyses, and causal models—are discussed in the following section. References to further, detailed explanations of the specific techniques are given in the second section of the bibliography.

JUDGMENTAL ESTIMATES. Some degree of judgment is implicit in all estimates, but, when statistical data are limited, the opinions of knowledgeable observers must be the basis for the forecast. Opinions are derived from experience, which is itself a form of historical data, and the experiences of industrial operators (for example, manufacturers, distributors, salespeople, bankers, consultants) are often a reasonable basis for the projection of market dynamics. Experience is even more valuable when taken from a systematic sampling of industrial experts. The most common judgmental forecasting methods are the following:[17]

- *Sales-force composite.* The sales estimates of individual salespersons are pooled into an aggregate sales forecast.
- *Executive jury.* The managers from different functional areas of the enterprise (for example, marketing, production, finance) jointly prepare sales estimates.
- *Panel consensus.* A group of industrial experts discusses and develops a common opinion and prediction.
- *Delphi.* The opinions of experts are gathered by questionnaires and the results are returned to the experts iteratively until convergence is approximated.
- *Cross-impact analysis.* The forces that will likely affect the forecast are identified, and experts systematically assess the effects of these forces on each other and on the forecast.

17. Definitions are drawn from an excellent literature review by Vithala R. Rao and James E. Cox, Jr., *Sales Forecasting Methods: A Survey of Recent Developments* (Cambridge, Mass.: Marketing Science Institute, 1978), appendix A, pp. 88–94.

TIME-SERIES ANALYSIS. Time-series methods relate sales to time rather than to causal factors that may underlie sales performance. They use historical data to identify and project past patterns and trends. These methods involve fitting a curve to the data and include free-hand, semi-average, least-squares, and trend-line projections.

In projecting trends, analysts should note the seasonal, secular, cyclical, and random variations. This is particularly important for agroindustries, which often face considerable price variability both seasonally and across years. Historical statistics can be adjusted to be more representative. For example, sales for a particular period can be estimated by using a moving average of preceding months. Time series can be separated into seasonal or cyclical trends. Similarly, data can be weighted differently through exponential weighting—for example, by assigning higher weight to years that are thought to be more representative of future trends. These methods all represent various kinds of moving averages and include simple, weighted, exponential smoothing, and the Box–Jenkins autoregressive moving average (which also employs weighting techniques). Decomposition techniques are also used to dissect time-series data into constituent elements. These time-series methods may be defined as follows:[18]

- *Free-hand projection.* The analyst plots the historical time-series data and projects them linearly.
- *Semi-average projection.* The analyst divides the series in half, calculates the average of each, and connects the two averages on the graph.
- *Least-squares curve fitting.* The analyst fits a curve to the time-series data by minimizing the squared error between the actual observations and the estimated curve.
- *Mathematical trend curve projection.* The analyst fits a known mathematical curve (with established properties) to the time-series data.
- *Simple moving average.* The analyst weights past observations by $1/n$; as new observations are made, they replace older ones in the calculation of revised averages.
- *Weighted moving average.* Same as in simple moving average, except that the analyst attaches different weight to different observations based on their expected predictions.

18. Ibid.

- *Exponential smoothing.* Same as in weighted moving average, except that the analyst uses a set of weights that decreases exponentially, thereby giving more recent observations more weight.
- *Box–Jenkins method.* The analyst uses an autoregressive, moving-average linear model to express forecasts as a linear combination of past actual values (or errors).
- *Classical decomposition.* With this method the analyst decomposes a time series into seasonal, cyclical, trend, and irregular elements.

CAUSAL MODELS. Causal techniques attempt to identify those variables which predict sales behavior. Regression analysis is one example of a causal technique that improves the accuracy of estimating. Simple regression uses one variable to predict sales, whereas multiple regression uses several—for example, population, growth, income, and price. The relations between the variables and sales can be plotted, and the points can be connected by a regression line. The relations can be calculated mathematically by the least-squares technique, which minimizes the sum of the squared deviations of the points from the line. Although regression analyses can be performed manually, inexpensive computer-program packages are also available to facilitate the task. It can be seen from the earlier example of the proposed Ghanian tinned milk factory that future sales could be estimated (from the data in table 2-3) by eye (judgmentally) or by using a formal regression analysis. These alternatives are demonstrated in table 2-5 through a comparison of a consultant's estimates with those of regression analysis. The differ-

Table 2-5. *Alternative Estimates of per Capita Tinned Milk Consumption in Ghana, 1964–68*
(ounces)

Year	Consultant's judgment	Regression analysis
1964	44.75	45.97
1965	46.75	48.72
1966	48.50	51.48
1967	50.25	54.24
1968	52.00	56.99

Note: Projected from consumption data in table 2-3; 1 fluid ounce = 29.573 milliliters.
Source: EDI, *Tinned Milk Market Forecast,* p. 7.

ence of approximately 10 percent in the 1968 projected volumes could have a significant effect on the firm's finances and capacity requirements.

Regression analysis is commonly used to determine demand, with price or income changes, by deriving elasticity coefficients. Elasticity estimates can be calculated from cross-sectional data from family expenditure surveys. The elasticity coefficient, e, is expressed mathematically as:

$$e = \frac{\Delta Q/Q}{\Delta P/P},$$

in which Q is quantity demanded and P is price. The change in sales resulting from a change in price is an indicator of consumer price sensitivity. When the percentage change in demand is greater than the change in price (a coefficient greater than 1.0), the demand is elastic. When the reverse is true, the demand is inelastic. When the two changes are equal and produce a coefficient of 1.0, there is unitary elastic demand. When elasticity is less than 1.0, demand is said to be inelastic. The concept of elasticity is also applied to demand changes that are a result of income changes.

Econometric methods attempt to measure the relations between several variables assumed to be demand determinants and to specify the degree of confidence that can be placed in those relations. Several sets of regression equations are used. The three aspects of econometric demand models are identifying the variables, specifying the relations, and making the projections. These models integrate the relations of multiple variables in the estimate; thus, they more accurately reflect reality. The main causal methods may be defined as follows:[19]

- *Simple regression.* The analyst statistically relates one possible explanatory variable to sales.
- *Multiple regression.* Same as above, except that more than one explanatory variable (with intercorrelations) is used.
- *Simultaneous equation systems.* The analyst uses a set of interdependent regression equations.
- *Input-output analysis.* The analyst uses a system of linear equations that indicates which inputs are needed to obtain certain outputs.

19. Ibid.

EVALUATION OF TECHNIQUE. The project analyst should evaluate the forecasting technique because each method is appropriate to different circumstances. The marketing manager should balance the cost of the technique against the desired accuracy to select the forecasting method. The requirement for accuracy is derived from factors such as the amount of capital being used, the firm's familiarity with the market, the uncertainty of demand factors, and the degree of risk decisionmakers are willing to take. (An entrepreneur might be satisfied with lower accuracy than might the banker considering a loan to the project.)

The success and accuracy of any forecasting method is dependent on the reliability of the data. Sophisticated econometric models and mathematical techniques cannot correct weaknesses in the original data. For example, econometric models are no more accurate than time-series analyses when structural changes are occurring in the economy.[20] Project analysts who are not economists should not be intimidated by demand equations. Rather, they can examine data and assumptions and let the mathematical analysts verify the estimating technique. Finally, analysts should recognize that a product may need different forecasting techniques at different points in the PLC, and that forecasting should be adjusted accordingly.[21]

Thus, the criteria for selecting a forecasting method are several and will depend upon the particular needs, resources, and data and product situation of the specific user. Among the likely criteria would be the method's cost, accuracy, skill and data requirements, and speed. As an illustration, these criteria are applied in table 2-6 to rank the various forecasting methods discussed in this section.

Salient points for project analysis

Demand forecasting is fundamental to the marketing analysis. The project analyst should consider the following questions when reviewing demand forecasting.

---

20. S. Makridakis and S. Wheelwright, "Forecasting: Issues and Challenges for Marketing Management," *Journal of Marketing*, vol. 41, no. 4 (October 1977), pp. 24–38.

21. For a further exposition of this need, see John Chambers, Salinder Mullick, and Don Smith, "How to Choose the Right Forecasting Technique," *Harvard Business Review*, vol. 49, no. 4 (July-August 1971), pp. 45–74.

Are the data on which the forecasts are based sound?
- Price data consistent?
- Units of measure standardized?
- Data disaggregated by market segment?
- Secondary sources exhausted?
- Type of primary data?
- Data-collection technique?
- Representative data?
- Data verified?
- Underlying assumptions of data?
- Sales and profit sensitive to changes in assumptions?

Table 2-6. *Evaluation of Forecasting Methods*

Method	Cost	Accu-racy	Skill require-ment	Data require-ment	Speed
Judgmental					
Sales-force composite	L	L	L	L	H
Executive jury	M	M	M	M	M
Panel consensus	M	M	H	M	M
Delphi	M	M	H	M	L
Cross-impact analysis	H	M	H	H	L
Time-series					
Free-hand	L	L	L	L	H
Semi-average	L	L	L	L	H
Least-squares	L	L–M	L	L	H
Mathematical curve	L	L–M	L–M	L	H
Simple moving average	L	L	L	L	H
Weighted moving average	L	L	L	L	H
Exponential smoothing	L	L–M	L	L	H
Box–Jenkins	H	H	H	H	M
Decomposition	M	M	H	M	M
Causal					
Simple regression	M	M	M	M	M
Multiple regression	M	M–H	H	H	M
Simultaneous equation	H	H	H	H	L
Input-output	H	H	H	H	L

L, low; M, medium; H, high.
Note: These rankings and the weights of the criteria can vary with the specific situations of individual firms or projects.

Are the forecasting methods appropriate?
- Source of judgmental estimates?
- Basis of source's expertise?
- Other opinions possible?
- Time-series data representative?
- Consideration of seasonal, secular, cyclical, and random variations?
- Regression technique?
- Estimates of price and income elasticity?
- Variables used in econometric model?
- Causal relations assumed in model?
- Rationale for variable selection and causal assumptions?
- Acceptable level of accuracy?
- Cost and value of increasing accuracy?
- Applicability of previous forecasting methods?
- Data and skill requirements of methods?
- Speed of conducting forecast?

Summary

Consideration of the marketing factor is vital to project analysis because it provides the market information to assess a project's viability. Too frequently, a firm's substantial efforts and investments are put into mounting procurement and processing operations—the other two of agroindustry's three main areas of activity —only to have the expected benefits never materialize because of an inadequate marketing analysis. Systems analysis views these main activities of an agroindustrial project as closely interdependent. This method identifies similar, closely related components in marketing analysis.

Because projects enter preexisting markets, it is essential that firms know the market environments. Accordingly, marketing analysis should examine consumers and competitors. A consumer analysis should identify consumer needs, potential market segments, and the buying process. For this analysis, the firm must conduct market research. A concomitant analysis of the competitive environment should describe the market structure, the basis of competition, and the institutional constraints affecting competition.

From analyses of the consumer and competition, a firm formulates its project's marketing plan. The plan should enumerate the project's marketing strategy for product design, pricing, promotion, and distribution. These elements of the marketing mix should be integrated in a comprehensive strategy that will place the product in an optimal marketing position relative to consumers' needs and competing products. The marketing plan should also consider the rest of the company's product line as well as the company's organizational, financial, production, and procurement operations to ensure the cohesion of the project's strategy. Once a marketing plan is adopted, the firm should anticipate the competitive reaction and formulate a response that will maintain the project's viability in a dynamic market environment.

The marketing analysis uses and is developed with the demand forecast. Analysts should consider the type, sources, reliability, and underlying assumptions of the data used in the forecasts. There are various forecasting methods such as judgmental estimates, time-series analyses, and causal models, and each is appropriate to different conditions. The analyst should determine how much accuracy is desired of the forecasting and balance this finding with the cost of using more sophisticated estimating techniques. Although project decisionmaking occurs under uncertainty, sound forecasting can reduce the ambiguity. Skill and data requirements and the speed with which the forecast can be made are additional considerations in selecting appropriate methods.

3

The Procurement Factor

IN THIS CHAPTER THE FOCUS of analysis shifts from the marketing of outputs to the procurement of inputs. The marketing and procurement activities of an agroindustrial project should be carefully studied before a company invests in a processing plant. Agroindustries transform inputs; if those inputs are defective, processing and marketing will suffer accordingly. In addition, because raw materials are the dominant cost to most agroindustries, the procurement system is a major determinant of the project's economic feasibility. Procurement is also critical to the project's effect on development because it links the industrial and agricultural sectors: by transmitting the market stimuli to the farmer, the procurement system directly affects rural families.

Primary Elements

There are five characteristics of an effective agroindustrial procurement system that provide a solid foundation for the processing operation. Procurement should be able to supply an adequate quantity of raw material of an acceptable quality at the appropriate time for a reasonable cost, and a system's success at achieving these objectives depends greatly on its organization. These primary elements to be assessed in the analysis of an agroindustrial project's procurement operations are examined in this chapter; stated in brief detail, they are as follows:

- *Quantity.* The analyst identifies output determinants and competing uses for the raw material.
- *Quality.* The analyst examines requirements of the marketplace, quality determinants, and quality control.
- *Time.* The analyst assesses the constraints of seasonality, perishability, and availability of raw materials.

- *Cost.* The analyst investigates the economic importance of the raw materials, cost determinants, and pricing mechanisms.
- *Organization.* The analyst examines the composition of the project's procurement system, its structure, power, vertical integration, and producer organization.

Adequate Quantity

Agroindustries frequently have excess capacity because they fail to ensure that an adequate supply of raw material will be available. The analyst should examine the determinants of output and the alternative users of the raw material with whom the processor will be competing.

Output determinants

The first step in analyzing the raw material supply is to examine the principal production determinants—area planted and crop yields.[1] For current crops, field surveys or trade sources give indications of the area and yield. For an indication of supply trends, production statistics should be examined by region over several years, and the forces affecting area and yield variables should be considered. The analyst will then be able to judge whether the historical production trend will continue and to assess the project's design in relation to the supply trends.

One of the factors affecting land area is the prevailing and expected land-use pattern. The analyst should calculate the actual cultivated land area and the arable but unused land; this latter estimate should be of "economically arable" land or land that can be cultivated with the economic resources likely to be available. Trends in land expansion should be examined because area increases can be the source of significant growth in supply. In Brazil, from 1947 to 1965, yields increased little, if at all, but outward migration in frontier areas almost doubled crop area.[2] The analyst

---

1. For livestock, production determinants are herd size and procreation rates.

2. John H. Sanders and Frederick L. Bein, "Agricultural Development on the Brazilian Frontier: Southern Mato Grosso," *Economic Development and Cultural Change,* vol. 24, no. 3 (April 1976), pp. 593–610.

should recognize, however, that new land may be of marginal quality and may produce lower yields.

Land, the basic asset in agriculture, has multiple uses. Hence, a farmer has several planting options. Analysts should examine the extent to which farmers switch among crops (or livestock) for an indication of the yearly supply variations in the crop (or livestock) needed by the processing plant. Because some farmers are restricted to one or two crops by soil or rainfall conditions or tradition, variability can often be reduced.

The analyst should consider the nutritional consequences to the country when farmers change crops to supply the processing plant. For example, switching from corn to a condiment crop might decrease the national supply of a staple, thus increasing its price (assuming no imports) and decreasing consumption by low-income consumers.

In areas surrounding major urban centers, farmland can also be used for urbanization and industrialization projects. Industrialization not only absorbs land but also bids away labor. For example, one fruit and vegetable processor found that farmhands and farmers began to change their occupations as automobile manufacturing plants located to the area. After several years the area became dominated by part-time farmers (see table 3-1). The number of farmers had declined by 28 percent between 1949 and 1967, with

Table 3-1. *Distribution of Full- and Part-time Farmers after Location of Automobile-manufacturing Plant in Baden-Württemberg, Federal Republic of Germany, 1970*

Farmers	Farms		Acreage[a]	
	Thousands	Percent	Thousands	Percent
Full-time				
(100 percent of income)	12	4	930	22
Part-time				
More than 50 but less than				
100 percent of income	121	42	2,420	57
Less than 50 percent of				
income	156	54	867	21
Total	289	100	4,217	100

Source: Otto Strecker and Reimar von Alvensleben, "The Unterland Corporation (B)," in Case Study no. 4-372-252 (Boston: Harvard University, Graduate School of Business Administration, 1972).

a. An acre = 0.405 hectares.

the decline in small-to-medium farms more prominent. These changes had a significant effect on the processor's procurement system because producers' economic interest in farming decreased, in turn decreasing raw material supply. Furthermore, economies of scale in production were prevented by the fragmentation of land. It is clear from this example that shifting land-use patterns can jeopardize a processing operation. The analyst should, therefore, examine industrialization and urban expansion programs.

Similarly, the analyst should examine agrarian reform projects being planned for the producing regions under consideration. Some reforms can significantly affect processors and it is advisable for land-reform planners to coordinate the market-outlet benefits of their project with agroindustrial development. Conversely, agro-industries should try to support reform efforts to ensure an adequate supply of raw material.

When analyzing yields, the analyst should concentrate on farm-input usage and techniques of cultivation (or animal husbandry). In general, the use of agrochemicals (fertilizers) and improved seeds (or breeds) will significantly increase yields even when the project is constrained by land availability. The analyst should determine the extent to which agrochemicals are presently being used by producers of raw material. The examination should also study the barriers to increased usage that accompany a particular project design. For example, one barrier to input usage might be that the agrochemical distribution channels were limited in geographical coverage or in the provision of financing to farmers for purchasing these inputs. Such barriers are common when raw material suppliers are small, traditional farmers. By identifying these barriers, the analyst can explore potential solutions—for example, improving the existing input supply ch..nnels, having the processing plant provide inputs to farmers, or organizing farmers to acquire needed inputs collectively.

It is not enough, however, to verify that the farmer will receive the inputs. It is critical that farmers also know how to use them— lack of knowledge has consistently been a major barrier to farmers' use of inputs. A national survey of small farmers in Mexico revealed that a majority did not use agrochemicals and improved seeds and that the primary reason for nonuse was an uncertainty and lack of knowledge regarding these inputs (table 3-2). This barrier indicates the need to identify the technical assistance required by the plant's potential suppliers. In general, small farms

Table 3-2. *Use and Primary Reasons for Nonuse
of Agrochemicals and Improved Seeds
by Small-scale Farmers in Mexico, 1973*
(percent)

| | | Reason for nonuse | | |
| | | *Uncertainty and lack of* | | |
Input	*Use*	*knowledge*	*High cost*	*Other*
Fertilizer	26	53	37	10
Herbicides	13	66	18	16
Improved seeds	16	74	19	7
Insecticides	23	61	25	13

Source: Compañía Nacional de Subsistencias Populares (CONASUPO) (Mexico City, 1973).

receive little technical advice, whereas larger farms heavily use agrochemical inputs and technical assistance. For example, in the Mexican study only 4 percent of the traditional farmers received formal technical assistance, a figure that reflects both the dichotomies between modern and traditional and commercial and subsistence agriculture and the inequalities in land and income distribution. If an agroindustrial plant is to increase its supply of raw material by improving farm technology, it may have to stimulate government agencies or input suppliers to provide farm assistance or it may have to offer technical assistance independently. Although the plant should encourage reforms in the structure of land tenure, these changes generally occur slowly.

The fundamental factor in the farmer's choice of which crop to plant or livestock to raise is economic, involving the weighing of alternative prices, costs, risks, and profits. The agroindustrial supply analysis should examine these assumptions, which affect a farmer's decisions, to make the projections of raw material supply. This examination is discussed further in the section on "Reasonable Cost," below.

Raw material supply is uncertain because of the variables inherent in agronomic production. The project analysis should, therefore, include a "supply sensitivity analysis" to measure the effect on total output of changes in area planted and crop yields. If there are no government or enterprise programs to stimulate output, the analyst should use historical planting and yield variations to determine the probable size of future crops. The wider the range, the greater the project risk, and the firm should consider such methods of reducing the risk as the importing of raw materials.

The sensitivity analysis can also be used to evaluate methods of increasing the supply of raw material. For example, when a cucumber-pickling plant was proposed in a Caribbean country, raw material requirements were computed as follows. The plant capacity, calculated on market demand estimates, was 60,000 10-ounce jars per day for 250 working days, with each jar containing 8 ounces avoirdupois or 0.5 pounds of fresh cucumbers.[3] During the pickling process, the firm expected a raw material damage loss of 15 percent. The total raw material requirement is computed below. Given that

Q_p = unit quantity of final product processed each day,
Q_r = quantity of raw material contained in each processed unit,
Q_d = number of production days,
L = percentage of raw material lost during processing, and
R = total raw material requirement,

then the total raw material requirement can be computed as follows:

$$R = (Q_p \times Q_r \times Q_d) \div (100 - L).$$

Substituting the particulars of the pickling plant's estimated capacity [R = (60,000 jars × 0.5 pounds a jar × 250 days) ÷ 0.85] obtains 8,824,000 pounds. Examination of the cucumber supply finds that the area planted in cucumbers had been fairly steady (±5 percent) for several years, at 1,200 acres with an average yield of 6,000 pounds per acre (±10 percent annual variation).[4] According to this finding, the expected average output is 7.2 million pounds and the processing plant's need is 8.8 million pounds, a shortfall of 1.6 million pounds from the previous calculation. If the shortfall cannot be eliminated, the plant will have to operate at 18 percent below capacity, a decrease that could significantly affect the plant's profit and the project's viability.

Assuming that equipment design cannot be adjusted to reduce capacity, the alternatives are to increase the area planted in cu-

3. One ounce avoirdupois = 28.349 grams; 1 pound = 0.453 kilograms.
4. One acre = 0.405 hectares.

cumbers or to improve the yields on the existing area. The analyst therefore needs to compute the amount that planting or yields would have to increase to equal the raw material deficit. Given that

R = total raw material requirements (8.8 million pounds),
A_a = actual area planted (1,200 acres),
Y_a = actual yield (6,000 pounds),
A_d = desired area planted, and
Y_d = desired yield,

then the desired area for planting can be calculated as follows:

$$A_d = R \div Y_a.$$

Performing the mathematical operations (8.8 million pounds ÷ 6,000 pounds) obtains 1,470 acres.

The desired yield from the actual area may now be computed as follows:

$$Y_d = R \div A_a.$$

Substituting the quantities in the equation (8.8 million pounds ÷ 1,200 acres) obtains an added yield of 7,333 pounds required to make up the shortfall. In other words, plantings will have to increase by 22 percent (to 1,470 acres) or yields will have to improve by 22 percent (to 7,333 pounds) to cover the deficit in raw materials.

These figures do not reflect a clear solution because they indicate equal rates of required improvement. The next step, then, is for the analyst to estimate the cost of each approach. To increase plantings, the firm will have to offer a higher price for the cucumbers to entice other farmers to cultivate the crop. To improve the yields, the firm will have to provide inputs such as improved seeds, agrochemicals, or technical assistance from an agronomist.

To compare the cost of each alternative realistically, the analyst must also consider the uncertainty of each method. To carry the supply sensitivity analysis one step further, the analyst estimates the probability of achieving the output by the alternative methods of increased acreage or increased yield. The uncertainty is important because it can reverse a decision based on cost comparison. Cost comparison, without considering uncertainty, would proceed as follows. If it is assumed that

C_a = incremental price per pound to induce increased planting ($0.02 a pound),

C_y = cost per acre of input package to raise yield ($175 an acre),

TC_a = total cost of increased planting, and

TC_y = total cost of improved yield,

then the option of increased planting can be assessed, using R (or 8.8 million pounds) from the previous calculations, by the following:

$$TC_a = C_a \times R.$$

Substitution ($0.02 × 8.8 million pounds) obtains a total cost for increased planting of $176,000. Alternatively, the total cost of improved yield can be calculated, using A_a (or 1,200 acres) from the previous calculations, by the following:

$$TC_y = C_y \times A_a.$$

Substitution ($175 × 1,200 acres) obtains a total cost of $210,000. Given that $TC_a < TC_y$, the firm should choose the increased planting alternative by this analysis. The elasticity of the cucumber supply, however, is unclear: the firm does not know how responsive farmers will be to the price increase. Having consulted the historical statistics on farmer price sensitivity, the analysts are 60 percent sure that the $0.02 added to the procurement price of a pound of cucumbers will stimulate increased plantings. Yet, conversely, they are even more certain of achieving the required yield increases because the desired yield (Y_d) of 7,333 pounds is the average yield in the United States, where climate is less favorable, and because small experimental plots in this Caribbean country have previously been shown to produce—under field conditions with the proposed inputs—consistent yields of over 8,000 pounds an acre. With this knowledge, the analysts attach a 0.9 probability to achieving a Y_d of 7,333 pounds and inflate the costs accordingly:

$$TC_a = \$176,000 \div 0.6 = \$293,333, \text{ and}$$
$$TC_y = \$210,000 \div 0.9 = \$233,333.$$

Another procedure would be to reduce the quantity of additional output generated by the alternatives and then divide by the original cost to obtain a cost per pound of the cucumbers expected to be procured:

$$TC_a = \$176,000 \div (8.8 \text{ million pounds} \times 0.6) = \$0.033, \text{ and}$$
$$TC_y = \$210,000 \div (8.8 \text{ million pounds} \times 0.9) = \$0.027.$$

Both calculations favor the yield-improvement alternative, a conclusion that is the opposite of the calculations made without the uncertainty factor.

Probability estimates are a rudimentary method of handling uncertainty factors in supply. More sophisticated analyses can be done with Bayesian probability theory and econometric modeling techniques. Demand forecasting techniques (discussed in chapter 2) are, to a great extent, applicable to supply forecasting. Regardless of the technique used, the analyst should consider the uncertainties surrounding supply procurement and include them in the analysis. Failure to extract judgments about uncertainty is common in agroindustrial project analysis; such failure means that these uncertainties either remain hidden or are treated unsystematically in the analysis or that they are simply forgotten. Neither of these alternatives is desirable if the quality of project analysis is to be improved.

Increasing the area planted and the yields are not, of course, mutually exclusive options. Supply sensitivity analysis should assess the combined effects of changes along both dimensions, a combination illustrated in figure 7. In examining projections of increased production, the analyst should ascertain the likely response from both because the feasibility of these two paths can vary dramatically. For example, land might be in abundance and traditional farmers might be resistant to new agronomic technologies. Under these conditions, the desirable strategy would be to increase supply by increasing crop acreage. If land were scarce, the analyst might choose the alternate method of increasing yields.

It is not feasible for those agroindustries that depend on other industries for raw materials to increase their raw material supply by the methods described above. Examples of such agroindustries are leather processors and shoe manufacturers that purchase hides from slaughterhouses or vegetable-oil processors that obtain cottonseed from gins. In these, the raw material supply is not influenced by the leather or oil processors but responds to the market demand of the primary products, beef and cotton. Consequently, the supply sensitivity analysis must focus on the productive capacity and market trends of the primary products. A deteriorating primary market often lowers production and the by-product processor has a short supply because of factors beyond its control. The processor should anticipate shortages and consider substitute raw materials or external sources.

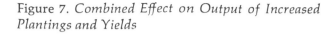

Figure 7. *Combined Effect on Output of Increased Plantings and Yields*

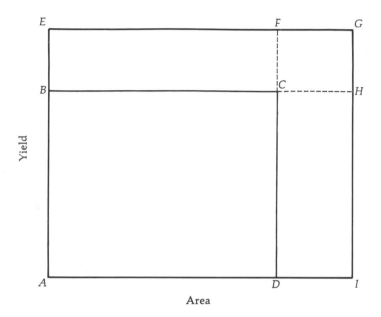

ABCD, Original output; *AEGI*, new increased output; *BEFC*, portion of increase from yield improvement; *DCHI*, portion of increase from larger plantings; *CFGH*, portion of increase from combined effect of improved yields and larger plantings.

Competing uses of raw material

After an examination of production determinants, the second step in analyzing the supply of raw material is to estimate the amount that will be available for the project's use. The analyst's task is to identify and qualify the relative uses of the crop to estimate the net quantity available to the proposed processing plant. Net availability is computed as follows:

> Gross production
> — On-farm consumption
> — Fresh consumption
> — Animal consumption

— Other industrial uses
— Competitors' purchases
— Losses
_____

= Net availability.

Each of these deductions from gross production of raw material is discussed below.

ON-FARM CONSUMPTION. One early crop deduction is that quantity which does not enter the commercial market but is consumed on the farm. In general, the more important the raw material to the diet of the rural population and the smaller the farm, the greater is its proportion of on-farm consumption. A subsistence farming pattern, however, may simply reflect the lack of a ready cash market outlet. If there is a market opportunity, a greater portion of the crop may be sold. If the market opportunity causes a crop switch from staple to cash crop, the nutritional well-being of farm families (as well as of landless laborers) may suffer. This possible effect depends on the increased sales, the income and price elasticities of the families for food and nonfood items, and the prices of these goods. Accordingly, the analyst must project and monitor the effects of the processing plant's raw material requirements on the population's nutritional intake.[5]

CONSUMPTION OF FRESH VERSUS PROCESSED CROPS. Another deduction is for the portion of the crop that is consumed in fresh, rather than processed, form. Some agroindustries must compete against the market for fresh agricultural products, and the intensity of the competition and its variation according to consumer preferences should be assessed by the analyst. In Mexico, for example, 90 percent of tomato production is consumed fresh. Fifty percent is for the domestic market and 50 percent exported to the U.S. winter market, where tomatoes receive a premium price in the absence of U.S. production.[6] In the United States, however, 83 percent of the

5. See Richard Goldman and Catherine Overholt, *Nutrition Intervention in Developing Countries: Agricultural Production, Technological Change, and Nutrition Goals,* U.S. Agency for International Development, Special Study no. 6 (Cambridge, Mass.: Oelgeschlager, Gunn, and Hain, 1980).

6. Organization for Economic Cooperation and Development (OECD), "Tomatoes: Present Situation and 1970 Prospects" (Paris, 1968), pp. 11, 79.

tomato crop is processed into products such as ketchup, tomato paste, canned whole tomatoes, and tomato juice because consumer preferences and demand for processed tomato products are greater than for the fresh produce. In addition, processing eliminates perishability and allows the large U.S. summer crop to be sold throughout the year.

For some crops, the fresh and processed markets are complementary rather than competitive. For example, tomatoes that are damaged in appearance could not be sold fresh but could be processed for tomato paste. This maximizes a crop's recoverable economic value.

ANIMAL VERSUS HUMAN CONSUMPTION. An alternative use for some raw material is its conversion into animal feed. In some countries corn, wheat, or soybeans are used in this way. It is nutritionally inefficient, however, to use grain calories and protein to produce meat: fewer calories and protein are available in the meat than were consumed in the grain because of losses in the biological conversion process.[7] Meat-processing agroindustries should be sensitive to this nutritional deficit and recognize that governments may have to give priority to direct human consumption of grains, especially in the face of widespread caloric shortages.

OPTIONS FOR MULTIPLE INDUSTRIALIZATION. Some raw material can be used in several processed end products. For example, corn can be used to produce animal feed, oil, starch, margarine, mayonnaise, noodles, detergent, flour, or dextrose. Although one processor may often produce several of these various raw material derivatives, it can find itself in competition for the raw material with a processor producing a different derivative. The analyst can foresee this dilemma by documenting and quantifying the alternative end uses of the raw material.

COMPETING PROCESSING FIRMS. The most direct competition for raw materials is among processing companies in the same business, and the competition can come from foreign as well as domestic pro-

---

7. It takes about 4 pounds of grain to produce a pound of beef; the meat is a higher quality protein, but generally costlier and less available to the nutritionally needy segments of society. Furthermore, unless the caloric deficits are met, the relatively expensive meat protein will be metabolized for energy rather than growth requirements.

cessing enterprises. The following example illustrates why the analyst must assess the strength of competition for raw materials.[8]

In the mid-1960s the cottonseed-oil processors in one Central American country had a scarcity of raw materials. A new local plant had been built, increasing the total demand for cottonseed from 1.725 million hundredweight to 3.225 million hundredweight, an increase of 86 percent.[9] Japanese oil mills were also in the market and purchased 1.75 million hundredweight in 1966. Meanwhile, the cotton crop was leveling off. The result of the stable output and growing demand was an 18 percent jump in the price of cottonseed from $2.80 to $3.30 a hundredweight. The Japanese were able to pay premium prices because they could generate additional revenue by extracting extra linters from the Central American cottonseed (other countries' seeds had been more thoroughly cleaned because of more efficient ginning).

LOSSES. A final deduction can be assigned to crop losses from rodents, insect pests, and poor handling and storage. The last of these losses merits examination because it can, in large part, be prevented. Poor storage facilities can be responsible for a sizeable portion of losses, although reliable statistics are scarce.[10] The Food and Agriculture Organization (FAO) estimates production losses at 10–30 percent, depending on the crop and region.[11] Low-cost storage facilities on-farm or in the village can cut these losses by as much as 80 percent.[12]

8. Gordon Bond, "Scollay Square Associates (A)," Case Study ICH-13G238 (Boston: Harvard University Graduate School of Business Administration, 1968).

9. One hundredweight = 45.359 kilograms.

10. For a useful discussion of the economic aspects of food storage, see "Research into the Economics of Food Storage in Less Developed Countries: Prospects for a Contribution from U.K. Technical Assistance," Communications Series, no. 61 (Sussex: Institute of Development Studies, University of Sussex, April 2, 1971).

11. E. A. Asselbergs, "FAO Action Program for the Prevention of Food Losses," speech delivered to the Agribusiness Management for the Developed and Developing World Food System Seminar (Boston: Harvard University, Graduate School of Business Administration, May 31, 1978).

12. David Dichter and Associates, personal interview (September 20, 1977); for low-cost storage techniques, see South and East African Management Institute, "Workbook for East African Workshop/Training Course on Improved Farm and Village-Level Grain Storage Methods" (Arusha, Tanzania, February 1977).

Storage and handling losses are frequently the result of programs to stimulate production that fail to incorporate adequate storage for the increased output. For example, Nicaragua launched a program to modernize its rice industry that boosted production 146 percent during 1967–69. The government's grain procurement agency was then overloaded with rice. One government official commented: "We bought more rice than the existing milling, drying, and especially storage capacity could handle. We had to store rough, wet rice wherever we could find space, even in buildings with dirt floors."[13] The inadequacy of the storage facilities caused an approximate 50 percent loss in the value of the paddy rice. Clearly, an analyst's accurate estimate of the storage needs for new production programs can help to ameliorate such losses.

Salient points for project analysis

An examination of the quantitative adequacy of raw material supply is the logical starting point for the analysis of a project's procurement activities. Processing plants operating at less than planned capacity are all too common and costly in most developing countries. The cause of this diminished productivity is frequently an inadequate analysis of the quantity of raw material available to the processing plant. The analyst should consider the following questions when examining the quantitative aspect of raw material procurement for an agroindustrial project.

What was the total production pattern?
• Production levels in the past?
• Degree of variability?
• Causes of variability?

What is the usage pattern of the area planted?
• Variation in area?
• Area economically arable but uncultivated?
• New trends in opening land?
• Productivity of new land?
• Extent and feasibility of crop shifting?

13. James E. Austin, "Marketing Adjustments to Production Modernization" (Managua: Instituto Centroamericano de Administración de Empresas [INCAE], 1972), pp. IV–1, IV–2.

- Nutritional consequences of shifting?
- Effects of urbanization, industrialization, land reform?

What is the yield?
- Variability in yield?
- Causes?
- Extent of usage of agrochemicals and improved seed?
- Barriers to increased usage of inputs?

How profitable is the crop?
- Profitability relative to alternative crops?
- Cost structure relative to alternative crops?
- Perceived risk?

How sensitive is supply to production changes?
- Effect on output of changes in area planted?
- Incentives needed to increase acreage?
- Cost and probability of increasing yields?

Is the raw material a by-product of another agroindustry?
- Supply and market demand of primary product?
- Import supply available?
- Substitute raw material available?

What is the on-farm consumption?
- Portion of crop consumed before marketing?
- Effect of higher output or prices on commercial marketing?
- Nutritional effects of increased commercialization?

How is the product consumed?
- Fresh, processed, or both?
- Proportions and trends of consumption?
- Complementary or competitive uses?

What is the animal versus human usage?
- Animal, human, or mixed usage?
- Proportions and trends of usage?
- Governmental priorities?

What are the industrialization options for the raw material?
- Number of end products?
- Relative demand and price differentials?

Is there competition in procurement among similar agroindustries?
* Number of competitors?
* Size of their raw material needs?
* Their procurement methods?

What are the probable crop losses?
* From rodents, insects, handling, storage?
* Measures to reduce losses?
* Adequacy of on- and off-farm services and storage facilities?

Acceptable Quality

A firm should not only have an adequate supply of raw material, but the material should meet the qualitative requirements of the operation. Raw material of poor quality may yield a product of poor quality that can create consumer resistance and have long-range effects on the firm's market position.

Marketplace requirements

The analyst must decide qualitative criteria for the raw material the firm uses. These criteria depend on standards of acceptability in the consumer market. This correlation again illustrates the interdependencies of agroindustry: to analyze the supply segment, the analyst must examine the marketing segment; to determine the parameters for quality, the analyst must perform the consumer analyses discussed in the previous chapter. In that chapter it was indicated in the consumer analysis that market segments within the same market have different qualitative standards dependent on variations in consumers' buying patterns. Cucumbers produced in Guatemala are an illustration of this variation. If the produce is to be packed and exported to the United States during the winter, it will be entering a highly quality-conscious market, and the analyst should identify the qualitative characteristics that reflect the market's preferences.

For example, a Guatemalan cucumber-packing project exporting to this market would have to apply rigorous criteria for color, size, shape, taste, and general appearance to the local crop (in addition, the U.S. government imposes sanitary standards on imported produce). If the cucumbers were being grown for the local Guatemalan market, the standards for quality would be lower and consumers would, in fact, refuse to pay the premium price for produce of export quality.

Once the qualitative demands of the market are identified, the analyst must translate them into qualitative requirements for the raw material.

Determinants of quality

Several factors affect the quality of raw material, and they must be adjusted to attain the quality required by the marketplace. Three factors in particular deserve the analyst's attention.

INPUTS. The input that affects product characteristics and quality most significantly is the seed (or, for livestock, breed). Plant and animal genetics engineer the input to achieve desired characteristics. Genetic research, however, has sometimes concentrated on quantity or yield and not given adequate attention to quality. The early IR-8, high-yielding rice varieties are a case in point. Introduced in the Philippines because they promised dramatically increased yields, the new seeds did succeed in this respect, but the IR-8 varieties also had a shorter grain, higher milling breakage, and poorer cooking qualities than the traditional varieties. IR-8 rice was therefore sold at a discount, thus offsetting much of the revenue gained by its increased yield. Genetic engineering of subsequent IR varieties removed these qualitative deficiencies and retained the high-yield characteristic. Clearly, both quantitative and qualitative dimensions must be considered in any genetic design of inputs.

For agroindustries such as the Guatemalan cucumber-packing operation discussed above, seed selection is critical. Varieties have been developed that meet the shape, color, and taste preferences of the U.S. market, but a firm must test these varieties under the agronomic conditions of its growing area (it is advisable to test varieties for at least two crop cycles and in various locations). To attain product quality, firms should use additional inputs such as insecticides and fertilizer, but these inputs must be properly used to achieve the desired results.[14] For example, the early cucumbers exported from Guatemala were frequently yellowish rather than the green color preferred by consumers, a deficiency thought to be caused by improper application of fertilizer.

Desirable characteristics in raw material can also be dictated by the processing operation. For example, special varieties of cucumbers and tomatoes have been developed for processing that are different from those used for fresh consumption. Genetic engineering has addressed these demands, but, again, the demands of the market remain critical. Finally, the analyst should consider the nutritional quality of the seed because seed variety can significantly influence the final product's protein and micronutrient content.

HANDLING AND TRANSPORT. The handling and transport of the product can also significantly affect its quality, and this is particularly true of more fragile and perishable products. For example, cucumbers are fragile and perishable produce: rough handling can bruise them, excessive exposure to sun can burn them, and they can wilt during transport delays. Potatoes, in contrast, can withstand rougher handling. But more than the esthetic characteristics of produce are at risk after harvest. Nutritional quality can also be affected by postproduction procedures.

The factors that most affect nutrient retention in harvested fruits and vegetables are mechanical injury and the conditions of temperature and humidity during handling and storage. Mechanical injury causes structural disorganization of the tissues and facilitates the entrance of microorganisms to the produce, causing spoilage. Oxidative reactions (chemical and enzymatic) occur when the cellular structure is disrupted and lead to a rapid loss of vitamins A and C. Temperature and humidity conditions affect products when moisture is lost (wilting), and there is a simultaneous loss of vitamins A and C. Wilting and vitamin loss occur when fresh, leafy vegetables are stored at high temperatures, low humidities, or both.

Mechanical injury to produce can often be prevented. Bruising from harvesting can be minimized by harvesting in the cool night

14. For economic and ecological reasons, consideration should also be given to natural methods of pest control and use of organic fertilizer.

hours, by quick application of precooling, and by avoiding delays before shipment. Damage may occur during harvesting, grading, cleaning, washing, transporting, packing and unpacking, and sale in market. In addition to labor-intensive benefits to the project, use of labor rather than machines at appropriate stages of operation can avoid some of this damage. In-transit damage can also be minimized: the injuries that occurred in peaches hauled 100 miles on a truck with leaf suspension were reduced in a shipment of peaches hauled the same distance on a truck with air-ride suspension.[15] Wilting can be minimized in leafy products by shortening the time between harvest and shipment and by monitoring temperature and humidity in storage.

STORAGE. Product losses because of poor storage facilities were discussed in the section on "Adequate Quantity," above. Defective or insufficient storage can also affect the quality of the product remaining after losses from excessive humidity or heat or insect damage. Certain produce may need refrigerated storage to reduce perishability. Deterioration in nutritional quality can also occur during storage, and this will be discussed in the section "Inventory Management" in the next chapter (see also tables 4-7 and 4-8).

Examination of the quality of the raw material, transport, handling, and storage should lead the analyst next to consider measures of quality control.

Quality control

In addition to providing the farmer with improved inputs to increase yield, the processor should also consider providing inputs to improve quality, such as better seeds. To ensure that the inputs are used properly, the firm may again need to offer technical assistance and training and may also wish to consider providing farmers with such physical facilities as warehouses and dryers. The costs of these measures should be compared against the economic benefits from prices for improved quality.

At a minimum, the plant should provide suppliers with a clear idea

15. M. O'Brien and R. F. Kasmire, "Engineering Developments and Problems at Production Source of Fresh Produce," *ASAE Transactions*, vol. 15 (1972), p. 566.

of the qualitative specifications for the raw material. Some firms offer premium prices and penalty discounts to stimulate producers' use of inputs and cultivation techniques that improve the quality of raw material. Other firms inspect crops while they are growing to detect problems such as insect damage and to minimize loss of quality. Sometimes the plant must produce the raw material itself to ensure adequate quality control. This form of backward vertical integration will be discussed in the section "Organization of the Procurement System," below.

Salient points for project analysis

It is evident from the discussion above that quality is important in procurement. The analyst should consider the following questions when examining the quality of an agroindustry's raw material supply.

What are the market's qualitative requirements?
- Different segments' standards?
- Price premiums for quality?

What is the quality of the inputs for farm supply?
- Effects of seed varieties?
- Effects of agrochemicals?
- Farmers' knowledge of input usage?

How does handling and transport affect quality?
- Personnel adequately trained?
- Availability and quality of transport?
- Nutritional deterioration?
- Adverse changes in appearance?

How does storage affect quality?
- Type of facilities?
- Quality of facilities?
- Nutritional deterioration?
- Adverse changes in appearance?

What services can increase quality control?
- Inputs provided by processor?
- Cost?

- Increased quality control?
- Economic benefits?

What qualitative specification and inspection procedures should be instituted?
- Standardized specifications for raw material?
- Communicated to farmer?
- Inspection procedures?

What quality control would result from backward vertical integration?
- Additional control?
- Cost versus benefits?

Appropriate Timing

Time is an important factor shaping the agroindustrial procurement system because of the biological nature of the raw material. The major characteristics that depend on time are the raw material's seasonality, perishability, and period of availability. Each of these characteristics merits brief discussion.

For seasonality

A primary timing problem in procurement is that most crops and range-fed cattle are seasonal; the procurement process is complicated because of the biological dictates of the crop and estrous cycles. Ideally, the raw material would flow from the field to the plant at an even pace or be adjusted to meet the prevailing pattern of demand. Such flexibility in supply is not possible in agroindustries; a farm does not have a nonagricultural firm's advantage of working the "production line" double time. Nonetheless, there is some flexibility. The crop cycle can be lengthened or shortened by planting the appropriate seeds, and irrigation can allow double cropping. Intensive feeding will reduce and spread the cattle-growing period, and planting can be staggered to spread the harvest period and thus lower the processing operation's peak capacity requirements. These adjustments, however, may be costly and difficult for the processor to obtain.

Even with such adjustments, storage is the prime regulator between the production and transformation of raw material. Storage absorbs the concentration of raw material and channels it into the processing operation as it is needed. Although external storage capacity and services may exist, the agroindustrial plant usually will also need to provide its own storage. The storage capacity required by a firm can be determined by computing the cumulative flow needed during the harvest period to meet the firm's annual requirements of raw material. As an example, the flow of raw material and the utilization of milling capacity for rice in Thailand are shown in table 3-3. Smaller mills have lower storage capacities and steadier milling rates throughout the season than do larger mills. Differences in the nature of the businesses are responsible for the discrepancy: the small mills provide services primarily to farmers who store their paddy rice at home and bring it for milling as they need to consume it, whereas the large mills buy the rice from farmers at harvest time, mill it, and resell it. Thus, the nature of the business also determines when a crop is supplied.

For perishability

Raw materials are perishable in varying degrees. Some materials must be processed immediately or the product suffers a significant loss in quality and economic value. For example, the nut oil from the African palm must be processed within a few days of picking or it acidifies and cannot be used. Similarly, if cucumbers are not harvested during the few days they are mature, they rapidly become oversized and unfit for exporting. The time of harvest can affect nutrient content, and postharvest delays can cause nutrient losses. For example, vine-ripened tomatoes contain approximately 40 percent more vitamin C than tomatoes picked green for subsequent ripening in storage.[16] Perishability places great importance on harvest programming and the scheduling of farm-to-factory transport and the analyst must determine whether transport services and scheduling are adequate to the resources of suppliers.

16. J. M. Krochta and B. Feinberg, "Effects of Harvesting and Handling on the Composition of Fruits and Vegetables," in *Nutritional Evaluation of Food Processing*, 2d ed., ed. R. S. Harris and Endel Karmas (Westport, Conn.: Avi Publishing Co., 1975), p. 98.

Table 3-3. *Seasonal Usage of Rice Mills in Thailand, 1975*
(metric tons daily)

Quarterly actual input	Capacity									
	0–10	11–20	21–30	31–40	41–50	51–60	61–70	71–80	81–90	91–100
February–April	0.63	6.47	11.63	18.61	25.75	35.32	48.29	38.00	40.00	58.12
May–July	0.67	3.76	7.28	14.21	14.30	32.50	31.57	35.67	30.00	50.63
August–October	0.40	2.32	5.61	8.39	11.88	25.05	23.14	29.00	30.00	40.00
November–January	0.59	2.26	5.77	5.74	7.93	20.27	24.14	24.50	30.00	28.75
Average	0.57	3.70	7.57	11.74	14.96	28.28	31.78	31.79	32.50	44.38

Source: D. Welsh and others, "Thailand Case Study," in *Global Malnutrition and Cereal Grain Fortification,* ed. James E. Austin (Cambridge, Mass.: Ballinger Publishing Co., 1979), p. 248.

The firm should attempt to decrease the risk from perishability if possible. For example, mechanical dryers can reduce grain humidity, thereby lowering the chances of stack burn and insect infestation; shaded collection points in the fields can prevent damage to fruits and vegetables from sun and heat. If perishability cannot be reduced, the firm might consider changing the form of the final product. A Central American producer of okra encountered severe problems in transporting the produce to the U.S. fresh market because transport delays were causing considerable deterioration and loss of the product. This producer countered these problems by installing a freezing plant and shifting to the market for frozen okra. The raw material could then be stored and was less perishable and time dependent.

For availability

There is an overall time period during which the raw material is available to the processing plant, the "life span" of the supply. The initial phase of this period is the length of time between the raw material's planting and the beginning of its flow into the factory. For commonly cultivated crops this first phase lasts only a period of months, but for new or unusual crops there is often a longer, trial growing period. For beef projects, a lead time is necessary to build up the herd so that a steady supply can flow to the factory. For African palms there is about a five-year lead time before the fruit can be harvested. Other fruit-bearing trees, tea, and coffee have similarly long lead times. Long start-up periods require special considerations for carrying the start-up costs of crops that are not generating any revenue.

The remaining phase of availability concerns the longevity of the raw material supply beyond its initial start-up period. Unlike minerals, crops are a renewable resource and can be planted again. Improper cultivation techniques, however, can lead to soil exhaustion or erosion whereby land becomes unproductive. The analyst should consider this longer-term availability and examine the cultivation techniques to ensure continuing supply. Tree crops have an extended but finite life, with an accelerating and then declining productivity pattern (the yield pattern of a Peruvian fruit and fruit-packing project, for example, can be seen in figure 8). Sequenced plantings can ensure an even and continued flow for the duration of productivity.

Figure 8. *Peach and Apple Orchard Yields, Valle de Majes, Peru*

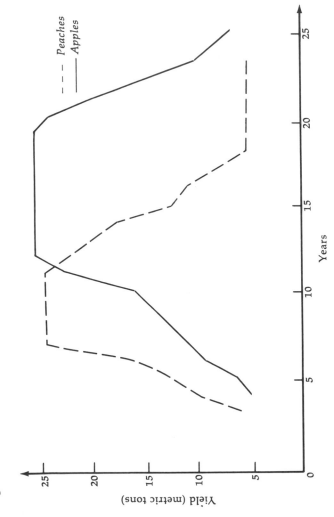

Source: World Bank, "Projecto Agro-industrial de Fruticultura para el Valle de Majes" ["Agroindustrial Fruiticulture Project for the Majes Valley"], Agricultural Projects Course Field Report, Arequipa, Peru (Washington, D.C., May 1976; a restricted-circulation document).

A crop's availability can be jeopardized when suppliers switch to other crops. This risk is especially acute when the raw material is a by-product of another crop, as is cottonseed oil (see the sub-section "Competing processing firms" in "Adequate Quantity," above). The supply of cottonseed depends on the demand for cotton; when cotton prices fall, farmers shift to other crops and seeds are less available. Because cottonseed represents a negligible portion of cotton farmers' revenues, a cottonseed-oil processor's increasing seed prices would not be an effective stimulant to increase cotton production. This lack of control again suggests the advantages of a firm's diversifying its sources of raw material: the firm processing cottonseed oil could, for example, explore the use of peanuts, soybeans, or palm kernels as supplementary oil sources. Diversification of this kind frequently requires adaptations in the processing equipment, and the analyst should compare the costs of modifying equipment with the benefits of having multiple sources of raw material, bearing in mind that multiple sources also reduce the risks of crop failure in one raw material or particular geographical area.

Salient points for project analysis

The following questions are important to the analyst examining the timing of the procurement system.

What is the seasonal harvesting pattern?
- Period of harvest (or time of slaughter)?
- Effect of seed (or livestock breed) on timing?
- Effect of planting (or feeding) on timing?
- Costs and benefits of changing the harvesting pattern?

What facilities are required by the seasonal pattern?
- Drying (or corral) capacity?
- Storage capacity for peak inventory?
- Availability of rentable storage space?

How perishable is the raw material?
- Timing of harvest (or slaughter) to prevent deterioration?
- Period after harvest (or slaughter) to avoid deterioration?

What facilities are necessitated by the raw material's perishability?
• Harvesting, transport, and storage?
• Scheduling?
• Special treatments to reduce perishability?

When and for how long will the raw material be available?
• Crop (or breed) new to area?
• Agronomic testing period?
• Planting-to-harvest period (or breeding cycle)?
• Farmer financing during start-up period?
• Ecological viability of agricultural practices?
• Pattern of life-cycle yield of perennial crops (or breeding stock)?
• Effect of flow of raw material on continuity?
• Switching among land uses expected?
• Effect of multiple sources?

Reasonable Cost

Not surprisingly, raw material costs dominate the economics of most agroindustries. Agroindustries usually do not perform an additive process, such as the assembling of components, as do other manufacturing enterprises. As a transformative operation, food processing is usually subtractive, reducing the original material. Its main additional inputs are labor, ingredients, and packaging. The costs of raw material in various agroindustries are illustrated in table 3-4. As shown in the table, raw material costs constitute from 54 to 92 percent of the total cost of projects. Because of the central importance of raw material costs, the analyst should explore alternative pricing mechanisms and test the sensitivity of profits to cost changes.

Cost determinants

Several factors—including supply and demand, opportunity costs, system structure, logistical services, and government interventions—affect the cost of the raw material, and these are examined in turn.

Table 3-4. *Importance of Raw Material Costs in Agroindustry*

Agroindustry and location	Raw material as percentage of total project cost
Beef processor (Brazil)[a]	92
Dairy (Brazil)[a]	67
Garlic and onion dehydrator (Ecuador)[b]	92
Meat processor (Yugoslavia)[c]	76
Poultry processor (Ghana)[d]	60
Soybean-oil refinery (Mexico)[e]	81
Sugar refinery (Ecuador)[f]	63
Wheat mill (Philippines)[g]	54
Winery (Yugoslavia)[c]	82

Sources: a. World Bank, "Brazil: Agroindustries Credit Project" (Washington, D.C., June 14, 1973; processed); b. World Bank and Inter-American Development Bank [IDB], "Proyectos agro-industriales de deshidratación de ajo y cebolla" ["Garlic- and Onion-dehydration Agroindustrial Projects"] (Washington, D.C., October 1974; processed); c. World Bank, "Appraisal of an Agricultural Industries Project—Macedonia" (Washington, D.C., April 30, 1973; processed); d. Business Promotion Agency Ltd., "Feasibility Report on Integrated Poultry Project" (Accra, n.d.); e. Fondo de Garantía, Development for Agriculture, Livestock, and Aviculture, "Planta extractora de aceites" ["Oil Extraction Plant"] (Mexico City, September 1973); f. World Bank and IDB, "Ingenios azucareros—Cuenca de Guayas" ["Sugar Refineries—Guayas River Valley"] (Washington, D.C., August 1974; processed); g. E. Felton, "Republic Flour Mills" (Manila: Inter-University Program for Graduate Business Education, 1977).

SUPPLY AND DEMAND. The major determinant of raw material cost is the supply and demand for the commodity. For demand, the analyst should assess the economic strength of the competing users of the raw material (see "Adequate Quantity," above). When supply is scarce, it will go to the firm that bids the highest; but, whether there is scarcity or abundance, the analyst should estimate the effect of the project's demand. The project's size is particularly relevant in this respect because the larger the project, the more it will disrupt the equilibrium of supply and demand. Large requirements for a raw material can strain supply and exert an upward pressure on price. If a project is the dominant buyer of a raw material, it may create a semimonopsonistic market position in which the enterprise becomes a pricesetter rather than a pricetaker. Although this would reduce the project's raw material costs, it might also have negative effects on the income of the farmers and their nutritional well-being if they are small, low-income producers. Seller-buyer power relations clearly need examining, and these will be discussed in the section on procurement organization, below.

OPPORTUNITY COSTS. One of the limitations to buyer power and influences on raw material prices will be the opportunity costs to the farmer who supplies a particular agroindustrial product. The analyst must determine what the farmer's crop flexibility is and then compute the profit of alternative crops relative to the profit of the crop the agroindustry requires. Although the project is not investing in agricultural production, it is still necessary for the firm to understand the farmer's economics.[17]

SYSTEM STRUCTURES. Structural factors in the farm-to-factory chain can also influence raw material costs. The most common of these is the middleman who buys the product from farmers and then sells it to the factory. There is a tendency to label these intermediaries automatically as exploiters and to consider their presence in the food system as undesirable. There is, of course, much evidence justifying such labeling, and intermediaries certainly have at times exercised oligopolistic control over supply channels. But these middlemen usually perform essential functions such as assembly, transport, or financing that someone else would have to perform in their stead if they did not exist. The analyst should determine the costs of these intermediary services and compare them to the costs, efficiency, and equity of alternative methods— for example, direct farm-gate procurement by the factory or direct delivery to the factory by farmer cooperatives.

LOGISTICAL SERVICES. Service costs can significantly increase raw material costs. Transport, a particularly important service charge, is often superficially analyzed or overlooked. Because raw material prices are often calculated to include delivery to the factory door,

17. For a practical approach to farm-level financial analysis, see J. Price Gittinger, *Economic Analysis of Agricultural Projects* (Baltimore: Johns Hopkins University Press, 1972), pp. 130–55. See also Howard N. Barnum and Lyn Squire, *A Model of an Agricultural Household: Theory and Evidence,* and Maxwell L. Brown, *Farm Budgets: From Farm Income Analysis to Agricultural Project Analysis,* World Bank Staff Occasional Papers, nos. 27 and 29, respectively (Baltimore: Johns Hopkins University Press, 1979).

the transport charges are not apparent. For example, a sugar mill in a Latin American country wanted to reduce the cost of the raw cane it was purchasing from small farmers because world sugar prices had plummeted drastically, putting the mill in a cost-price squeeze. The mill dropped the price to the farmers from $7.00 per ton delivered to the factory to $5.00, a price it considered still profitable for farmers. Consequently, a large portion of the farmers began to shift to different crops, threatening the mill's supply of raw material. Examining the farm-to-mill cost structure (see table 3-5), the mill found that transport charges had absorbed over 40 percent of the farmers' revenue at the old price and were absorbing 60 percent at the new price, thus making the farmers' operation at the new price unprofitable. The mill invested in a fleet of trucks that it could operate at one-third the cost of the previous trucking service, thus preserving the farmers' returns and lowering the delivery cost of the cane. Alternatively, the producers could have collectively set up a transport service.

GOVERNMENTAL INVOLVEMENT. It is often necessary to trace costs through the farm-to-factory chain to uncover the effects of government programs. For example, the poultry-processing industry in an African country ultimately traced costs back to the feed-grain farmer to find the cause of—and government responsibility for—price increases in its raw material. The government was concerned about the high price of broilers because the poultry industry had been considered a means of providing less expensive animal protein

Table 3-5. *Illustrative Cost Structure of Sugarcane Production and Delivery in a Latin American Country, 1972*
(U.S. dollars per metric ton)

Item	At old price		At new price	
	Cost	Percentage	Cost	Percentage
Price paid by mill to farmer	7.00	100	5.00	100
Charges paid by farmer to transporter	3.00	43	3.00	60
Wages paid by farmer to worker	1.50	21	1.50	30
Land costs paid by farmer	1.00	15	1.00	20
Net return to farmer	1.50	21	—0.50	10

Source: Author estimate based on unpublished company documents.

to the lower-income segments of the population. The high retail prices of broiling chickens led the government to contemplate instituting price controls on poultry meat to eliminate excessive profits to processors. But, when the policymakers traced the cost components from retailer to processor to poultry farmer, they found that processors' profit margins were not excessive and that the primary cost factor was poultry feed (see table 3-6). Taking the analysis further, they found that the feed mills were also operating on thin profit margins and that the real source of the high cost of feed was the high, prevailing support price for feed grains, which the government itself maintained. Given the economic dominance of this raw material in the industry, high prices at the end of the chain were inevitable. Yet the high support prices were not stimulants effective enough to increase grain output. This suggests that there were other production constraints, such as inadequate

Table 3-6. *Illustrative Cost Structure for Broiler Chicken Agroindustry in an African Country, 1973*
(U.S. dollars)

Item	Cost per chicken	Percentage
Retailing		
Retail price	3.24	100.0
Markup	0.25	7.6
Processing		
Dressing	0.20	6.1
Packaging	0.05	1.5
Distribution	0.10	3.0
General and administration	0.15	4.6
Profit margin	0.15	4.6
Growing		
Incubated chicks	0.20	6.1
Feed	1.80	54.7
Disease control	0.05	1.5
Mortality	0.05	1.5
Maintenance	0.04	1.2
Transport	0.10	3.0
Profit margin	0.15	4.6

Source: Author estimate based on unpublished industry studies.

credit or technical assistance, that would have been more appropriate objectives for government action.

Pricing mechanisms

It is clear that many forces influence the cost of a plant's raw material. The analyst can consider various alternatives, the following among them, for the plant's obtaining its raw material at a reasonable cost.

SPOT PRICES. Buying at spot prices means the company pays the prevailing price in the market. This is a reasonable procedure if the competitors also use it because all firms incur similar costs. Prices, however, tend to vary greatly both annually and across years, thereby causing uncertainty in financial planning.

MULTIPLE SOURCES. When using spot prices, it is desirable for the firm to have multiple sources of raw material. This permits the procurement officer to shift the mix of raw materials, thus achieving the best cost and helping to control price variability and the economic risk of dependence on one crop.

SUPPORT PRICES. Sometimes it is necessary for the firm to pay the minimum commodity price as fixed by the government. Although this may be a deviation from the price that would have prevailed under free-market supply and demand, support prices are often appropriate because they represent the farmers' opportunity costs.

CONTRACTING. One method of ensuring the supply of raw material is to extend purchase contracts to producers. Such contracts often specify delivery quantities, quality standards, delivery dates, and price. Price is the most problematic of these because, in spite of the contract, a firm has pricing options. The spot price upon delivery could be used, but the firm and the supplier would have to agree on what the source of the spot price should be. The contract could also fix the price on a cost plus a fixed fee or margin. Another possibility would be to base the price on opportunity costs, thus to minimize crop shifting and to stabilize supply. Yet another alternative would be to pay a base price plus a variable bonus derived from the final prices of the processed products. In examining these various contract alternatives, the analyst should compare the costs against the certainty obtained under each.

Firms might accompany contract pricing with ancillary benefits such as the provision of technical assistance or advances of working capital to suppliers. Working capital requirements for purchases of raw material and for storage are an important dimension of procurement operations and should be given special attention in project analysis.

Project analysts should also consider the length of the contract. Long-term contracts based on fixed prices may be convenient to producers and processors because they increase economic certainty and facilitate financial planning, but both the benefits and the risks of variability under spot pricing are avoided by this kind of contracting.

Long- or short-term, contracting is effective only as long as external conditions do not significantly alter the underlying economics of the contracts. Such alterations affected the cotton industry of a Central American nation in 1973. In May 1973 many cotton farmers had sold forward contracts to Japanese buyers for approximately $39 per hundredweight of lint cotton. By January 1974, however, world prices had soared to $86 per hundredweight, and farmers refused to honor the contracts because their input costs had risen because of higher agrochemical costs and because they wanted a share in the higher world prices. The government finally intervened with a compromise whereby the farmers had to deliver 70 percent of their contracts at the original prices but could receive the world prices for the remaining percentage.[18]

The value of contracts ultimately depends on the goodwill of the parties involved. Legal enforcement is often not feasible because of the costs and delays of adjudication, and contracts may need to be flexible enough to presume the benefits as outside conditions change.

JOINT FARMER-PROCESSOR VENTURES. Another method of achieving reasonable costs for raw material is to invite producers to invest in the industrial plant, thus giving them a vested interest in the success of the processing operation. This may not, however, always be the result. In one dairy plant the suppliers, who were also shareholders, maintained their producer interests by demanding higher prices for their raw milk. Because they perceived the processing

18. For more details on this case, see Kenneth L. Hoadley, "The Nicaraguan Cotton Case" (Managua: INCAE, 1974).

firm's profitability as unimportant, they drained the dairy of its retained earnings; it was unable to maintain or modernize its equipment and, consequently, fell into disrepair and financial difficulty.

BACKWARD INTEGRATION. Instead of buying from farmers, the agroindustrial enterprise should consider integrating backward to produce some or all of its raw material. For some products this is highly economical and will reduce raw material costs. The earlier example (see "Logistical services," above) of a sugar mill that organized its own transport fleet illustrates effective backward integration. Cost, however, is not the only consideration in deciding on integration; others will be discussed in the section "Organization of the Procurement System," below.

Sensitivity analysis

The cost of raw material varies according to several market factors. Because raw material costs are uncertain yet are the dominant product cost for an agroindustry, it is necessary that the project's financial analysis include a "sensitivity analysis of raw material cost" to determine the effect of variations in raw material prices or profits and investment returns.

The analysis should be analogous to the "price sensitivity analysis" illustrated in chapter 2. The example of the spice manufacturer from that chapter (see the subsection "Data assumptions") illustrates the financial implications of changes in raw material costs. Of the plant's total annual costs of $300,000, 82 percent, or $246,000, was attributable to the raw material. Thus, if the price of raw material increases 10 percent, total costs rise 8.2 percent and profits drop 12.5 percent. A 20 percent increase in raw material prices would consume one-quarter of the firm's profits. Conversely, if raw material prices drop, profits would increase. The analyst can assess the effect of such variations and calculate an expected cost for raw material. A full sensitivity analysis would integrate the variations in both the sales of finished goods (see table 2-4) and the cost of raw material. A combined sensitivity analysis of this kind is shown in table 3-7.

Salient points for project analysis

Even if an agroindustrial firm can obtain an adequate quantity of quality raw material, the firm will not be profitable unless the

Table 3-7. *Sensitivity Analysis of Sales and Raw Material Costs*
(U.S. dollars)

Item	Historical trend holds	Raw material costs rise 10 percent	Revenues fall 10 percent	Costs rise 10 percent and revenues fall 10 percent
Revenues	500,000	500,000	450,000	450,000
Costs	300,000	325,000	300,000	325,000
Profits	200,000	175,000	150,000	125,000
Change in profits (percent)		−12.5	−25	−37.5

raw material's cost is reasonable. The analyst should therefore consider the following questions in examining the cost of the procurement system.

How do supply and demand affect the cost of raw material?
• Strength of demand from competing users?
• Effect of project on demand and prices?
• Availability of supply at different prices?

What are the farmers' opportunity costs?
• Alternative uses of land?
• Relative profitability of alternative uses?

How do structural factors affect costs?
• Margins of middlemen?
• Cost and feasibility of factory's performing these functions?

How do logistical services affect raw material costs?
• Existing transport charges?
• Contribution of transport to prices?

How does governmental involvement affect raw material costs?
• Price supports?
• Import or service subsidies?

Should spot prices be used?
• Prevailing spot prices?
• Variability during and across years?
• Competitors' buying practices?

Are multiple sources a potential pricing mechanism?
• Multiple crops for the raw material feasible?
• Relative price levels and variability?
• Lowest cost combination?
• Organizational or technical problems?

How do governments' support prices affect pricing?
• Existence of support prices?
• Portion of crop affected?
• Comparability with spot prices?

Is contracting a potential pricing mechanism?
• Current use of production contracts?
• Duration of price agreements?
• Expected contract compliance?

Are joint ventures feasible and desirable?
• Farmers interested in investment?
• Effects on raw material costs?

Would backward integration lower raw material costs?
• Feasibility of integration?
• Effect on costs?

What does the sensitivity analysis of raw material costs reveal?
• Effect of raw material cost changes on profits and return?
• Probability of such changes?

Organization of the Procurement System

Obtaining an adequate supply of quality raw material at the appropriate time and for a reasonable cost ultimately rests on the organization of the procurement system. This organization can be examined through the system's structure, channel power, vertical integration, and producer organizations.

Structure

In the section "Adequate Quantity," above, it was suggested that the projected supply of raw material could be computed from production statistics. But there is a difference between statistical and actual supplies. Unless there is an organizational structure between farm and factory, the potential supply to the factory may never be realized. In one Southeast Asian nation a modern, multimillion-dollar beef-processing plant was constructed. The project analysis included national statistics that revealed a large and growing cattle population. Six months after opening, however, the factory was operating at only 8 percent of capacity because it lacked raw material. Contrary to the project analysts' expectations, the statistical cattle did not materialize as beef: the cattle owners were small farmers with transport problems who, because they were unaware of the plant's needs, did not, or could not, alter their custom of selling their cattle to the local abattoir or to middlemen who in turn sold to the abattoirs.

It is necessary to analyze the structure of the raw material's production and distribution to determine where and how the new project's procurement system will fit in. Several dimensions of this structure should be examined.

NUMBER OF PRODUCERS, TRANSPORTERS, BUYERS. Knowing the number of operators in the system will help the firm to evaluate methods of reaching potential suppliers. If the structure is fragmented and contains many small producers, the task of produce assembly and the organizational burden may be great. Analysis of the operators in the system will also help the firm to identify possible bottlenecks in crop assembly or transport and will suggest the competition in buying.

SIZE. When farms are large, the plant needs fewer suppliers. Large farms can also use a variety of production techniques, such as irrigation or mechanized harvesting, that can affect supply certainty and the processing plant's scheduling. Nevertheless, firms should be careful to avoid a bias against smaller farm suppliers, who can be excellent sources of raw material and who by their involvement can generate a greater socioeconomic developmental effect than can large suppliers alone. The issue is that suppliers of different size have different resources and production techniques that may require different services from the factory or government. For example, small farms may require transport services, whereas larger ones may have their own vehicles. Similarly, and with the appropriate technology, small farmers can make desired output gains.

Seeds and fertilizer are divisible inputs equally applicable to large and small farms if the project can ensure that financial and technical assistance are also available. In West Pakistan, for instance, small farmers adopted low-cost tubewell systems, suggesting that irrigation needs can also be addressed at the small-scale level.[19]

LOCATION. The firm must know the location of the producers in order to determine transport costs, optimal plant location, logistical control problems, and the vulnerability of supply to disease or drought (if these are geographically concentrated).

CROP MIX. The analysis should identify growers of specific crops and the relative market importance of these growers and crops to anticipate shifts by suppliers among them. Patterns of crop specialization will also be revealed by the analysis.

OWNERSHIP PATTERNS. The analysis should define land that is owned, rented, sharecropped, or squatted. Owners may be more willing than renters to adopt new cultivation techniques because of the fixed investments but, again, the project should make a conscious effort not to favor the land-owning farmers over the renters and thus to encourage the dichotomous agricultural structure. Financial incentives and land-reform programs may be necessary for the project to maintain this evenhandedness. Inequitable land tenure is a fundamental constraint on agroindustries' achieving their developmental potential.

FLOW. The analyst should also determine the quantity and sequence of produce flows through each operator in the procurement system. These distribution channels should be documented so the firm can determine whether the project can also use the existing flow system.

Analysis of channel power

Not only the structure of the procurement system must be understood, but its inner operations, including the system's power rela-

19. Frank C. Child and Hiromitsu Kaneda, "Links to the Green Revolution: A Study of Small-scale, Agriculturally Related Industry in the Pakistan Punjab," *Economic Development and Cultural Change*, vol. 23, no. 2 (January 1975), pp. 249–75.

tions, as well. To understand the procurement channels, one must locate the power and determine its base. Indicators of power are the size of profit margins, the volume of produce handled (as percentage of total marketed crop), and the number of participants involved in each intermediate step (for example, transporters, storage operators, industrial buyers). These data can be gathered by examining the procurement system's structure or by interviewing participants in the system.

Clearly, all participants in the system have some power. Farmers' power derives from their possessing the product buyers desire. Transporters' power comes from the service they offer. Financers' power is based on their critical input of capital. An agroindustry is powerful because, as a market outlet, it is a buyer. Sometimes the power in a channel derives from noneconomic factors such as personal or family ties. The analysis should focus on the system's relative distribution of power and its imbalances because the latter can create inequities, disruptions, and inefficiencies in a factory's procurement activities. The challenge facing an agroindustry's procurement operation is to achieve a "positive sum game," by which the new factory benefits, rather than exploits (a "zero sum game"), the participants in the system. If the new factory threatens to exploit the participants, they will resist the firm's entrance to the market. If small farmers are the injured participants, the project's social desirability is questionable.

A government may occasionally exercise monopolistic power through marketing boards or partially intervene through price supports and procurement programs of its own. In each case the government becomes the agroindustry's potential supplier.

Backward vertical integration

A major issue in designing the procurement system is whether the firm should use the existing producers or integrate vertically backward to assume some production, assembly, or transport functions. The advantages to vertical backward integration depend on the needs of each project. The analyst should, however, be aware of some of the possible effects of integration, which are briefly considered below.

CONTROL. If the agroindustry has adequately qualified people to perform the new functions, its control will increase with integration. Increased control improves the likelihood of the firm's obtaining the desired quantity and quality of raw material. Centralizing the decisionmaking should also improve product coordination and increase the dependability of supply.

CAPITAL REQUIREMENTS. Integration can significantly increase the fixed and working capital requirements cf the agroindustrial project, which in turn increase the project's costs and capital exposure.

FLEXIBILITY. Backward integration tends to lock the agroindustry into fixed investments and a predetermined structure. This limitation reduces multiple source options.

COSTS. An integrated system permits efficiencies and economies of scale that are not otherwise attainable and therefore allows the firm to achieve lower variable costs. But integration also implies greater fixed costs for the project: if market prices fall, these increased fixed costs can represent a significant expense to the project.

Although definitive guidelines for backward vertical integration are impossible, it is a more appropriate strategy than operating solely through existing channels when a firm is introducing a new crop or opening new production areas. This opening of new ground is what led Central American banana firms to develop from the start totally integrated structures for cultivation, packing, and export. There were no existing supply systems. A more common pattern of organizing sources, currently used by the banana industry, is to obtain a portion of the raw material from the factory's own farms and a portion from outside producers. Backward vertical integration may not be feasible because political constraints or blockages in channels may resist the concentration of power or because the possible labor displacement from integration may not be deemed socially desirable. Alternatively, the firm can use producer organizations, a strategy which has its own advantages.

Producer organizations

Recently, agroindustries have frequently served as catalysts for the collective organization of farmers. In the past, producers often failed to organize because they lacked a strong focal point around which to mobilize community interest and participation. By providing a new market outlet, agroindustries have also created a necessary economic incentive for farmers to organize.

The agroindustrial plant can encourage such organization by incorporating incentives in its procurement strategy. Farmers will sometimes organize without the plant's encouragement, especially if the plant has created a power imbalance in the farm-to-factory system. In one country, a new tomato-processing plant began purchasing the bulk of the local farmers' output. When the farmers became dissatisfied with the prices, they were motivated to form a cooperative; by consolidating their power, they were able to negotiate supply contracts with the factory at improved prices. Organizing producers, however, is a difficult and time-consuming task, and analysts should identify the barriers to organizing and the potential inducements to surmount them.

When the barriers are attitudinal, economic incentives are not sufficient. For example, one government launched a major program to increase its cattle supply. The farmers affected by the program were primarily rice producers, each of whom owned an average of eight cattle, which grazed freely on common land and the farmer's plot. Each farmer reared and sold the cattle as he chose. The government intended to form cooperatives, fence the common land, pool the farmers' cattle in large herds, and provide veterinary services and financing for tractors and inputs for new pastures. These components of the program were expected to decrease cattle mortality and morbidity rates, shorten the growth cycle, and raise the slaughter weight. When the program started, farmers refused to enter the cooperatives and pool their cattle because both concepts were dramatic departures from the farmers' traditional patterns of individual ownership and production. Even though the program was economically sound, it required too great a change in the producers' attitudes toward trust relationships and collective action, and its potential remained unrealized.

Producers' organizations can be advantageous to the agroindustrial plant, especially when procurement depends on numerous small suppliers. If suppliers organize, the plant has a conduit for communication and negotiation with farmers, a channel that can save the plant considerable effort, time, and money. It is organization that is advantageous. The processor should not presume that the smaller farms will be less productive simply because of their size; empirical evidence from developing countries indicates that "overall, an absence of economies of scale or changing total factor productivity with size seems to be typical."[20]

One effective method for a processor's initiating a producers' organization is for the processor to identify the multiple constraints surrounding the small farmers' efforts in produce marketing and then to suggest a solution. The most common marketing barriers include infrastructure (for example, roads and storage), services (for example, transport and shelling), inputs (for example, bags and credit), and information (for example, prices and market standards). Because the marketing system is also a social system, barriers from social obligations and behavioral patterns can also be expected.[21]

Frequently, several barriers must be confronted simultaneously before the market stimulus from the agroindustry can affect the farmer. This was the conclusion of CONASUPO (Compañía Nacional de Subsistencias Populares), the Mexican government's agricultural produce-marketing organization.[22] Although CONASUPO's support prices were higher than those of intermediaries, few farmers sold to the organization and, consequently, its warehouses had a tremendous excess capacity. A survey revealed that farmers lacked transport for their grain to the CONASUPO warehouses, adequate price information, bags, and shelling equipment; furthermore, the farmers had promised their crops to buyers who had lent them pre-harvest money. In response to these findings, CONASUPO mounted a program to reimburse farmers for the cost of farm-to-warehouse transport, with the farmers assembling their grains and locating the means of transport; to provide shelling services at cost; to lend

20. R. Albert Berry, "Cross-country Evidence on Farm Size/Factor Productivity Relationships," in *Small-Farm Agriculture: Studies in Developing Nations*, Station Bulletin no. 101 (West Lafayette, Ind.: Purdue University, Department of Agricultural Economics, Agricultural Experiment Station, September 1975), p. 20.

21. An instructive discussion of agricultural marketing constraints operative in rural Africa can be found in Uma Lele, *The Design of Rural Development: Lessons from Africa* (Baltimore: Johns Hopkins University Press, 1975; 3d printing, with new postscript, 1979), pp. 100–15.

22. James E. Austin, "CONASUPO and Rural Development: Program Description, Analysis, and Recommendation," consultant's report to World Bank (Washington, D.C., December 1976; processed).

bags to the farmers; and to provide consumer credit that would free the farmers from store owners and other middlemen.

In this case it was the government that developed a marketing system for the small farmers, but the processing plant could have done it. The Anand Cooperative, a producer-owned milk-processing plant in India, successfully incorporated hundreds of small farmers and landless rural dwellers as suppliers. By providing technical production inputs, a guaranteed market outlet, and fair prices paid upon delivery, the cooperative doubled the income of the landless laborers who comprised one-third of its members.[23]

These examples introduce a final aspect of procurement organization that merits consideration: a producer's forward vertical integration. Up to this point, this study has focused on the processor's integrating backward toward the producer. If, however, the farmers themselves integrate vertically forward to the processing stage, they can become the owners and operators of an agroindustry. Larger, wealthier, and more managerially sophisticated producers are more likely than small farmers to integrate vertically forward. Yet smaller farmers are not excluded from entering the processing stage; combining their efforts to form a cooperative or corporation, as discussed above, can lead to this integration. Producer cooperatives in the process of integrating vertically forward, however, frequently encounter managerial problems. An agroindustrial operation is different from farming, and the analyst advising such cooperatives should ensure that the producers have had adequate training, receive technical assistance, or obtain contracted, external management. A poorly managed agroindustry can become an economic burden to farmers if their production profits are only consumed by processing losses. Successful producers' cooperatives exist, but they generally have developed over time. The effective fruit-marketing cooperatives of Taiwan, for example, took thirty years to evolve.[24]

23. Michael Halse, "Operation Flood: An Introduction to the Study Papers on the Indian Dairy Development Program," Case Study no. 3-577-100 (Cambridge, Mass.: Harvard University, Graduate School of Business Administration, 1976).

24. Wen-fu Hau, "Development of Integrated Cooperative Export Marketing System for Bananas in Taiwan," Seminar on Marketing Institutions and Services for Developing Agriculture, September 10–12, 1974 (Washington, D.C.: The Agricultural Development Council, Inc., 1974).

Salient points for project analysis

Agroindustrial procurement systems can be organized in different ways and should be tailored to the needs of each project. Nevertheless, the analyst should consider the following questions when assessing a procurement system's organization.

What are the number, size, and location of the operators in the structure of the existing system?
- Number of producers, transporters, buyers?
- Implications for organization and control of system?
- Percentage of crop handled by each?
- Size of supplier and its interaction with plant?
- Supplier location?
- Implications of suppliers' location for plant's location, logistical control, and vulnerability of agronomic supply?

What is the suppliers' crop mix?
- Current crops?
- Extent of specialization?
- Degree of crop shifting?

What are the patterns of land ownership?
- Land ownership, renting, or sharecropping?
- Farmer mobility?
- Effects on plant's procurement relations?

What are the routes, timing, and accessibility of the raw material's flow?
- Channels?
- Size of flow?
- Timing of flow?
- Availability to plant?

What does the analysis of channel power reveal?
- Locations of power in system?
- Extent of power?
- Basis of power?
- Basis and strength of project's power?

Should producers integrate vertically backward?
- Added control over quantity, quality, and timing?

- Extent of integration?
- Additional requirements for fixed investment and working capital?
- Reduction of flexibility in obtaining sources of raw material?
- Effect on variable and fixed costs and break-even point?
- Political feasibility?
- Social feasibility?

Are there producers' organizations?
- Degree of producers' organization?
- Purposes and activities of producers' organizations?
- Barriers to organization?
- Possible incentives for producers to organize?
- Use of organizations to communicate, control quality, transmit services?

Should farmers integrate vertically forward?
- Financial and managerial resources available for, and economic and social benefits from, such integration?

Summary

Because of the transformative nature of agroindustries, the processing plant's input of raw material is critical. Defects in procurement and supply are carried through, and sometimes magnified in, the processing and marketing activities. Raw material costs are also, in general, the major cost of the agroindustry. Moreover, the organization of the project's procurement system can significantly determine its socioeconomic benefits.

The effective procurement system attempts to obtain a quantity of raw material that will satisfy both market demand and a plant's processing capacity. Defining that quantity requires an examination of the raw material's historical, current, and projected planting area, yields, and alternative uses. The raw material must also meet the desired qualitative requirements. Variable characteristics determine produce quality, and each market will have its own qualitative standards. It is essential for a plant to identify these quality requirements in its market(s) and to determine what characteristics of the raw material will produce the desired end product. The quality of raw material is affected by farm inputs, cultural practices, and storage and transport services. The plant will need quality-control mechanisms to monitor and upgrade its raw material.

In addition to obtaining the desired quantity and quality of raw material, the procurement system must also ensure that the raw material is delivered to the plant at the appropriate time. Timing is complicated by several factors. The seasonality of production, inherent in the biological nature of the raw material, causes an uneven flow to the factory. This cyclical pattern creates a peak flow, which requires extra processing or storage capacity. The agro-industrial firm should consider methods to spread the flow of raw material more evenly. The perishability of raw material similarly emphasizes the timing of the system's movement of produce from the farm to the factory. Storage and processing techniques can reduce losses to perishability. Availability—determined by the raw material's growth cycle and the expected duration of supply—also affects procurement timing. Before making the fixed plant investment, a firm should ascertain the certainty of supply and the relative permanency of the crop.

Although the quantity and quality of the raw material and the timing of its procurement may all be acceptable, the procurement system is not economically viable unless the raw material is reasonably priced. The cost must be low enough to allow the processing plant to generate a profit that yields an acceptable return on investment. The analyst must examine the main factors affecting costs: supply and demand, opportunity costs, structural factors, logistical services, and governmental interventions. The mechanisms and alternatives for establishing raw material prices should similarly be evaluated: spot prices, multiple sources, governmental price supports, contracting, joint ventures, and backward vertical integration. In addition, the analyst should calculate the sensitivity of profits and investment returns to changes in raw material prices.

The procurement system's overall effectiveness ultimately rests on its organization. To achieve this organization, the firm should begin by studying the farm-to-factory structure, which is built upon the number, size, and location of farmers, middlemen, transporters, storage operators, and other industrial buyers. The analyst should also examine the pattern of farmland ownership, existing degrees of vertical integration, and the volume and channels of commodity flow. This structural analysis leads to an examination of power within the supply channels, the basis of that power, and the implications such power holds for the project's raw material supply. The plant's major alternative to using the existing structure is backward vertical integration, and the desirability of this alternative should be assessed in relation to control, capital requirements, flexibility, costs, social effects, and political feasibility. Project analysts should also determine whether producers are, or could be, grouped into cooperative organizations and how such organizations would affect the agroindustry's procurement system. One last option analysts should explore in examining a project's procurement activities is the possibility of farmers' integrating vertically forward into processing.

4

The Processing Factor

THIS STUDY HAS PROGRESSED through an examination of agroindustrial output (marketing) and input (procurement) activities and will now assess processing, the transformative activity of an agro-industry. The processing stage is operationally central to an agro-industrial enterprise and the point at which project analysts must make crucial investment decisions.

Primary Elements

Processing operations for food and fiber vary widely in form and complexity with the kind of processing performed (for example, sorting or cleaning, mixing, milling, extraction, canning, freezing, drying, cutting, cooking, pasteurization; see table 1-1) and the kind of raw material (animal or plant) processed. (See appendix A and tables A-1 through A-3 on drying, freezing, and canning.) Despite such diversity, there are several common factors that should be considered when examining an agroindustry's processing stage. They include the following, each of which will be discussed in the sections of this chapter:

- *Selection of processing technology.* The analyst reviews the implications of market requirements; flexibility in processing; costs and availability of labor, capital, materials, and energy; nutritional consequences; and source considerations.
- *Plant location.* The analyst examines considerations of raw material, market, transport, labor, infrastructure, land, and developmental effect.
- *Inventory management.* The analyst assesses storage capacity, physical facilities, and financial aspects.
- *Supplies for processing.* The analyst identifies needs for inputs other than raw material.

- *Programming and control.* The analyst considers the design of production and quality-control systems.
- *By-products.* The analyst examines the economic possibilities of secondary outputs of production.

Selection of Processing Technology

Technology selection is often the most important decision in the design of the project's processing operation. The major criteria for selecting the technology are qualitative requirements, process requirements, socioeconomic cost, capacity utilization, management capability, and nutritional consequences.

Qualitative requirements

The processing technology to be selected for the project should be tailored to meet the market's requirements for product quality (as determined in chapter 2). Because consumers' preferences for quality vary, there is a range of technological options that will yield varying levels of desired quality in the agroindustrial end products. The firm can avoid unnecessary investments and maximize revenue by modulating its processing technology to the requirements of its selected market segments.[1] For example, in rice milling the major qualitative factor governing price is wholeness of the grain. The export prices of Thai rice in 1975 reflect this factor:

Quality (percent broken grains)	Price (U.S. dollars per metric ton)	Quality discount (percent)
0	345	0
5	303	—12
15	287	—17

1. Choosing a technology that will produce a quality superior to that in the market might be desirable as a competitive tool for increasing market share by meeting unmet preferences. Consumers' standards for quality are dynamic. The analyst should, therefore, assess the risk of the technology's becoming obsolete from changing qualitative preferences and ascertain means of improving quality to meet altered needs.

In milling operations, breakage is determined by seed variety and the kind of drying and milling equipment. Technological options range from pounding by hand to almost completely automated milling. The higher capital investments for more sophisticated technology must be compared with the higher revenues from the larger total milling yield and the premium prices that the increased yield of whole grain will obtain. The qualitative demands of the market and the price spread between whole and broken grain are one criterion for deciding on more or less sophisticated technology.

The qualitative requirements of the export market frequently exceed those of the domestic market. A production shift to exporting may require corresponding technological adjustments. Alternatively, the servicing of both markets may permit a broader use of raw material because products unacceptable for the export market can be sold domestically. Similarly, it may be desirable to operate both fresh and processed fruit and vegetable operations simultaneously. Produce that is unacceptable in the fresh market because of perishability (easy blemishing or early maturity) can be processed. For example, a marketing project for fresh apples in India added a processing component to use the culled apples, which represented 20 percent of its gross production, and significantly increased farmer income.[2]

Process requirements

Certain kinds of processing can only be carried out by a narrow range of technology because of the nature of the transformative process. Consequently, little choice exists regarding the type of equipment to be used. These technical constraints can also have economic implications. A capital-intensive process, for example, will have a minimum economic scale of operations, below which the agroindustry will not be financially viable. These possible requirements of scale must be assessed against the market forecasts to see if the project should proceed.

2. Arnold von Ruemker, "Reappraisal of Himachal Pradesh Apple Processing and Marketing Project (India) Case Study," Economic Development Institute (EDI) Case Study Exercise Series, no. AC-156-P (Washington, D.C., revised January 1977; processed).

Within the constraints imposed by the market and process requirements, the project attempts to select the technology that will
minimize costs. In calculating costs, however, the analyst should
consider public as well as private costs because they can differ
significantly. Different technologies can also make varying uses of
the factors of production. Thus, the analyst should examine the
relative scarcity and costs of these factors. The principal production
factors to be considered are labor, capital, energy, and raw material.

LABOR VERSUS CAPITAL. The tradeoff between factors most discussed in the debate over "appropriate technology" is the paradigm
of labor versus capital.[3] By this model labor is viewed as abundant
and capital as scarce; therefore, labor- rather than capital-intensive
technology should be used. Pools of surplus labor that face few
employment opportunities cause low opportunity costs. Accordingly, a shadow pricing of costs would favor the labor-intensive
technological option, especially when increased employment is a
social priority. But the wage paid by the factory may be higher than
the opportunity cost because of minimum wage laws, social benefits, and other factors. Furthermore, artificially low interest rates
or overvalued exchange rates may make the import and use of
capital equipment more financially attractive to the owner of the
factory than an intensive use of labor. (These "prices" could be
adjusted in the analysis of the social costs and benefits.) In this
case the public and private interests would diverge, and means of
reconciling these differences through policy adjustments or the redesign of the project would be in order.

There are, however, variations on the paradigm. C. Peter Timmer's analysis of alternative levels of rice-milling mechanization in
Indonesia will serve to illustrate.[4] Timmer concludes that a small
plant, milling four tons per hour and consisting of two machines
for hulling and whitening, is economically superior to hand pounding or to larger mills with mechanized drying and storage facilities
(see table 4-1). His conclusion may be debated, however, because
of the possible negative effects on employment and income distribu-

3. See the fourth section of the bibliography for additional references.
4. C. Peter Timmer, "Choice of Technique in Rice Milling on Java," *Bulletin of Indonesian Economic Studies*, vol. 9, no. 2 (July 1973), pp. 57–76;
reprinted as a Research and Training Network Reprint (New York: Agricultural Development Council, Inc., September 1974).

tion that the shift from hand pounding to small, mechanized mills might cause. Yet the shift away from in-house hand pounding may reflect the response of Indonesian mills to a strong consumer preference for convenience and time saving. The data in table 4-2 show that in-house hand pounding is uncommon in rice and maize processing in other countries.

One means of redesigning a project to increase its use of low-cost labor is to disaggregate the technology. This requires the plant to identify each step in the production process and to assess the use of manual labor for each activity. Frequently, the handling and sorting of materials can be carried out manually more cheaply than by mechanization. Packaging, in some instances, can also use labor rather than automation. Activities that require high precision or chemical transformation, however, can often only be done mechanically (that is, the process requirements limit factor substitution).

The disaggregation process also relates to economies of scale. The economics of capital-intensive investment rests in part on economies of scale. Large production units are essential to achieving high volume and low unit costs. Least-cost production for the total set of agroindustrial processes within an industry does not, however, necessarily exclude small-scale industries (ssi's). The firm should examine the agroindustrial system to identify the functions that are better performed by small-scale production units than by larger, capital-intensive units. For example, the leather and footwear industry in India comprises the processes of skinning, curing, tanning, finishing, and making. Skinning and curing are small-scale functions because of the nature of the procurement of the raw material: dead animals are found and skinned by numerous, individual entrepreneurs (the killing of cows being forbidden by religious beliefs). The tanning process requires large equipment and, therefore, high volume. The shoe- and leather-goods-making stage of the process, however, can be efficiently conducted on a small scale with a modest amount of equipment. The successful Italian shoe-export industry and Brazil's expanding shoe industry rely heavily on ssi's at the making stages. (These countries have an advantage over India in that cattle are slaughtered for meat and the raw material hides are of superior quality.)

Although some authors have asserted that labor-intensive technologies in practice are frequently inferior to capital-intensive ones because they use both more labor and more capital to produce the

Table 4-1. *Alternative Rice-milling Technology in Indonesia, 1972*

	Type of milling technology				
Technical and economic specification	Hand pounding (s)[a]	Small (s)[a]	Large (s/m)[a]	Small bulk (m)[a]	Large bulk (m)[a]
Data per unit					
Capacity (metric tons per year)[b]	n.a.	1,000[c]	2,500[d]	7,200	21,600
Investment cost (U.S. dollars)[e]	0	8,049[e]	90,511[d]	453,283	2,605,926
Operating laborers (number per shift)	n.a.	12[c]	16[d]	27	39
Data for 1,000 metric tons of rough rice input per year					
Investment cost (U.S. dollars)[e]	0	8,049	36,204	62,956	120,645
Operating laborers (number)	22.00[f]	12.00	6.40	3.75	1.81
Milled rice output (metric tons)	570	590	630	650	670
Market price (rupiahs per kilogram)	40.0	45.0	48.0	49.5	50.0
Value of output (millions of rupiahs)	22.8	26.6	30.2	32.2	33.5
Value added[g]	4.8	8.6	12.2	14.2	15.5
Data for 10 million rupiahs in value added per year					
Investment cost (U.S. dollars)[e]	0	9,359	29,675	44,335	77,835
Operating laborers (number)	45.83	13.95	5.25	2.64	1.17

n.a., Not applicable.

Source: C. Peter Timmer, "Choice of Technique in Rice Milling on Java," Bulletin of Indonesian Economic Studies, vol. 9, no. 2 (July 1973); reprinted as a Research and Training Network Reprint (New York: Agricultural Development Council, Inc., September 1974), p. 6.

a. The s in parentheses indicates that the facility uses sun drying; m indicates mechanical drying.

b. Milling capacity is measured in metric tons of rough rice input yearly, assuming the facility can operate 2,400 hours in a year.

c. The technical and cost data for the small rice mill relate specifically to a locally manufactured husker of the "flash" kind with an input capacity of three-quarters of a ton per hour, which is linked to a polisher of the Engelberg kind with an input capacity of half a ton per hour. A thresher shed and sun-drying pad are provided, but no additional storage capacity. This facility is taken as representative of the entire range of small rice-milling facilities.

d. The mechanical and cost data for the large rice mill relate specifically to a Japanese self-contained milling unit integrated with storage capacity for 756 tons of rough rice, 360 tons of bagged rice, and 456 tons of bulk rice in upright steel bins. A mechanical dryer with a capacity of three-quarters of a ton per hour is provided along with a sun-drying pad. The milling capacity is 1.0 to 1.1 tons of rough rice per hour. Costs of building and machinery (including a diesel-powered thresher), but not land, are included. In 1972, US\$1 = Rp413.

f. This assumes that one worker hand pounds about 150 kilograms of gabah (rough rice) daily, with a yield of approximately 95 kilograms of rice.

g. Value added is calculated assuming a gabah cost of 18 rupiahs per kilogram, which is above the floor price of 16 rupiahs per kilogram for "village dry" gabah at the mill. The cost (and value added) of reducing the moisture to "mill dry" gabah is included as a mill activity.

123

Table 4-2. *Patterns of Rice and Maize Processing in Thailand, 1975, and Guatemala, 1973*

Country	Percentage	
	Processed in mills	Pounded in home
Thailand		
(province)		
Ayuthya	100	0
Cahyaphum	88	12
Kalasin	100	0
Phichit	99	1
Phrae	99	1
Songkhla	85	15
Guatemala		
(region)		
Rural highlands	99	1
Rural East	98	2
Rural South	98	2
Semi-urban	99	1

Source: James E. Austin (ed.), *Global Malnutrition and Cereal Fortification* (Cambridge, Mass.: Ballinger Publishing Co., 1979).

same output,[5] there are many possibilities for increasing labor intensity without a firm's becoming economically inferior. Possible approaches to be considered by analysts would include the selection of labor-intensive production stages within the agroindustrial system, as in the example of the leather industries, above; the choice of products that are more labor intensive; or the separation of the unalterable aspects of technology, in which the substitution of capital for labor is dictated by process or market requirements, from the nonessential aspects, in which substitution is dictated by labor costs or management preferences.[6] The analyst should also realize that there are numerous technological options and machine-

5. See, for example, Richard S. Eckaus, "The Factor Proportions Problem in Underdeveloped Areas," *The American Economic Review*, vol. 50, no. 2 (May 1960), pp. 642–48.

6. For a Marxian perspective on substitution, see G. E. Skorov (Institute of World Economy and International Relations, USSR Academy of Sciences), *Science, Technology, and Economic Growth in Developing Countries* (London: Pergamon Press, 1978), pp. 87–94; for a critique of this perspective, see Deepak Lal, *Men or Machines* (Geneva: International Labour Organisation, 1978), Appendix A, pp. 59–62.

labor permutations for capital intensity. The wide variations in capital and variable costs that exist among similar or different processes are illustrated in appendix A. (The cost estimates provided in the tables of appendix A are reference data for costing comparable food-processing technologies.)

A project can often save significant capital—without sacrificing product quality or jobs—by purchasing used machinery. High labor costs in more industrialized nations put a premium on labor-saving innovations; hence, manufacturers purchase new machinery to compete. Although the equipment displaced by this practice is not economically viable in the industrialized market where it originated, it can be viable in the less industrialized nations. These nations have lower labor costs and are willing to install the labor-intensive equipment for both financial and social reasons. The used equipment does not alter the quality of the end product but simply takes advantage of the cost differentials between factors; what has become inappropriate technology for one environment can be quite appropriate for another. For example, a Colombian textile manufacturer visited by the author purchased a large equipment complex from a U.S. textile firm that was shifting to a newer, labor-saving technology. The capital savings to the Colombian firm from purchasing used equipment were sufficient to pay for the training of workers in disassembly and operation of the equipment, the freight costs, and the reassembly and installation of the whole equipment complex.

There are several reasons why secondhand equipment is not purchased more frequently. The information on the kind and quality of available equipment is frequently scarce, and the purchaser from a developing country may have to travel to the industrialized country to inspect the machinery. The supply of replacement parts for older machinery may be difficult to obtain.[7] Policymakers or plant engineers may psychologically view used equipment as "low status" or "unprogressive."[8] In this case, the analyst should remind

7. The analyst should verify the availability of parts and servicing (relative to costs and quality) of any imported versus local equipment, whether the imported equipment is new or secondhand.

8. Louis T. Wells, Jr., "Engineering Man vs. Economic Man," in Timmer and others, *The Choice of Technology in Developing Countries: Some Cautionary Tales*, Harvard Studies in International Affairs, no. 32 (Cambridge, Mass.: Harvard University, Center for International Affairs, 1975), pp. 319–42.

these parties that, in socioeconomic terms, new is not necessarily better. Used equipment is also difficult to appraise and, therefore, its purchase complicates the government's task of fiscal assessment. An alternative to buying secondhand equipment is the acquisition of technology by licensing, subcontracting, or direct foreign investment. This and other aspects of technology selection are documented in the fourth section of the bibliography.

ENERGY. Another factor of production to be considered in selecting technology, and one that is of increasing economic concern to both developed and developing nations, is the energy requirement of technology. Agroindustries use significant amounts of energy. In the United States, for example, energy use by food processors in 1975 accounted for 4.8 percent of all energy used (farm production alone accounted for only 2.9 percent).[9] Before committing itself to one technology and energy source, the agroindustrial firm should assess the supply and price of alternative fuels and the energy usage of various technologies (see tables A-1 through A-3). Rice, for example, can be dried by the sun or by machine (see table A-1). Solar energy is, of course, free, but the energy savings of this source would have to be weighed against other factors, such as the quality of the end product. Rice dried in the open air is subject to damage by insects or weather. If the alternative sources were coal, fuel oil, or wood, the product would have to be indirectly heated to avoid contamination by soot or smoke. If the alternative were natural gas, the cost might be greater but the processor could use direct combustion heaters, which have lower capital and operating costs and a higher efficiency. Sometimes energy is underpriced (subsidized) by the government. This is true in Saudi Arabia and has led certain private entrepreneurs to set up vegetable dehydration plants there. If the energy had been shadow priced at its opportunity cost to society, these projects would have shown a negative social cost-benefit ratio. Thus, the need to assess the social, as well as the financial, costs is as important for determining energy costs as it is for analyzing the labor and capital factors.

Procedures for "energy accounting" of food-processing opera-

9. Office of Industrial Programs, Federal Energy Administration, *Energy Use in the Food System* (Washington, D.C.: U.S. Government Printing Office, 1976).

tions have been developed. R. Paul Singh[10] has proposed that the analyst:

- Decide on an objective (for example, to improve the efficiency of thermal energy used in a process);
- Choose a system boundary (for example, a piece of processing equipment or a series of processing operations);
- Draw a flow diagram of the process (using standard symbols);[11]
- Identify and quantify all mass and energy inputs (for example, steam, heated air, or electrical energy that crosses the system boundary);
- Identify and quantify all mass and energy outputs (including any increase in energy incorporated in the product itself).

This accounting can generate alternative energy costs per unit of product for different technologies and fuel sources. It can also reveal points in the process that can benefit from alternative energy sources—for example, the use of solar energy to heat water required in processing. Food technologists or industrial engineers can provide the requisite calculations for the estimates in energy accounting.

An emerging source of energy for some countries is the agro-industrial production of ethanol from biomass.[12] Biomass-based ethanol is particularly useful as a gasoline substitute and as a chemical feedstock, and it can be produced from sugar-bearing materials, starches, or celluloses. The basic technology is well known, and sugarcane-based ethanol appears to be economic at oil prices of $31 a barrel. A major consideration, however, is that sufficient land be available for crops intended for ethanol pro-

10. R. Paul Singh, "Energy Accounting in Food Process Operations," *Food Technology*, vol. 32, no. 4 (1978), p. 40.

11. International Federation of Institutes for Advanced Study (Energy Analysis Workshop on Methodology and Conventions, 1974), in "Energy Accounting as a Policy Analysis Tool," Report to the Committee on Science and Technology, U.S. House of Representatives (Washington, D.C.: U.S. Government Printing Office, 1976).

12. For a more complete analysis, see World Bank, "Alcohol Production from Biomass in the Developing Countries" (Washington, D.C., September 1980).

duction and that this land not displace acreage needed for staple food crops.

RAW MATERIAL. For some agroindustries the scarcest resource may not be capital or energy but raw material. Consequently, priority must be given to that technology which makes most efficient use of the raw material. That raw material costs are the greatest expense for most agroindustries was indicated in the previous chapter. Because of this constraint, any technology that can produce cost savings here can yield a significant economic benefit.

Use of capacity

One of the common problems facing agroindustries is the underuse of capacity because of the seasonality of raw material availability and market demand for the product (for example, ice cream, chocolates, or certain beverages). To some extent, the kind of technology selected can reduce idle time caused by seasonal factors. Many processing steps are the same for different products requiring the same kind of transformation (see chapter 3, the subsections "Competing uses of raw material" and "For availability"). Consequently, a plant constructed to process beans, for example, can readily process certain other vegetables or fruits with modest additional equipment and changes in labor procedures. Similarly, dairies equipped for heat processing or canning could process tomatoes and pineapples.[13] By adjusting the technology to handle a broader range of products, agroindustries can procure raw materials over a longer period that encompasses the cycles of different crops.

Other means than technological exist for reducing the effects of seasonality; these include the planting of multiple crops through use of irrigation or new seeds; the achievement of shorter breeding cycles through animal genetics; the substitution of stored, semiprocessed raw material (for example, powdered milk; see the subsection "Storage capacity," below) in the production process; and the introduction of special advertising to consumers during the off

13. International Labour Organisation, "Labour and Social Problems Arising out of Seasonal Fluctuations of the Food Products and Drink Industries," Second Tripartite Technical Meeting for the Food Products and Drink Industries, Report no. 2 (Geneva, 1978).

season. Finding ways to increase full use of project capacity is important not only for increasing the revenue-generating period of the investment but also for reducing the adverse socioeconomic consequences of seasonal unemployment.

Management capability

Another criterion for technology selection is the fit of the technology with the enterprise's managerial resources. Managerial talent is often scarce in developing countries, particularly at the supervisory level. Technology selection can minimize the supervisory burden, perhaps by substituting machines for those parts of a process that require the most intensive supervision. (The qualifications regarding tradeoffs between capital and labor made earlier, however, would then apply.) Skilled technicians are also scarce, and so the maintenance and repair requirements of equipment must be carefully assessed. Highly sophisticated agroindustrial equipment has often ended up idle because of a plant's deficient maintenance capacity.

Nutritional consequences

A commonly overlooked criterion in technology selection is the processing method's effect on the nutritional value of food products.[14] In general, food processors have shown little interest in the nutritional content of their products because they have not thought that consumers consider nutritional value to be of major importance in their purchasing decisions.[15] Yet technology can have a significant effect on the nutritional value of foods, and the analyst of agroindustrial projects should give explicit attention to this aspect of technology selection. Food technologists and nutritionists can provide technical information for the analysis of a product's nutri-

14. The author expresses appreciation to Dr. Sam Yong for his research assistance in developing this section.

15. See James E. Austin, "Can Nutrition Sell?," *The Professional Nutritionist*, vol. 8, no. 3 (September 8, 1976), pp. 12–15; "Marketing Nutrition," *Cereal Foods World* (November 1977), vol. 22, no. 11, pp. 567–71; and *Confronting Urban Malnutrition: The Design of Nutrition Programs*, World Bank Staff Occasional Papers, no. 28 (Baltimore: Johns Hopkins University Press, 1980), pp. 36–43.

tional value, but, because of the relative neglect of the nutritional dimension in project analysis, it will be addressed here in some detail.

Food nutrients can be roughly divided into two categories, macronutrients (proteins, carbohydrates, fats) and micronutrients (vitamins, minerals). The constituents of these two categories, as well as the nutritional effects of various kinds of food processing, are discussed below.

PROTEINS. Processing can increase or decrease the digestibility of proteins. For example, heat-induced denaturation can enhance the general digestibility of foods, but heat can also reduce protein quality by degrading, or blocking metabolism of, the ε-amino group of lysine (especially in the presence of reducing sugars—for example, glucose, fructose, and lactose).

CARBOHYDRATES. Under normal processing conditions starch is stable, but reducing sugars may degenerate and simultaneously brown in the presence of catalysts and heat.

FATS. During processing and storage, isomerization and oxidation of fats may decrease the biological value of unsaturated fatty acids. The deterioration of fats—which is increased by heat, light, and the presence of trace metals—may cause losses in the organoleptic values of foods. Such deterioration may be retarded by the action of antioxidants that are naturally present in fats or that can be added to fats during processing.

VITAMINS. Some water-soluble vitamins—thiamin (vitamin B-1), riboflavin (vitamin B-2), niacin, pyridoxine (vitamin B-6), and ascorbic acid (vitamin C)—are lost during processing to an extent depending on their degree of solubility and stability, the kind of food, and the processing conditions. Ascorbic acid is readily oxidized during processing, especially in the presence of copper or iron at neutral pH. Thiamin readily degrades in neutral and alkaline solutions even at moderate temperatures and is also sensitive to heat, copper or iron, and sulfites. Riboflavin is stable except in the presence of light at neutral or alkaline pH. Niacin, probably the most stable vitamin, has excellent stability under heat and light. Pantothenic acid is stable at mildly acidic or neutral pH but more heat sensitive at acidic pH. The stability of folic acid depends partly on its chemical form: the monoglutamate form is moderately stable under heat at acidic or neutral pH, but the tri- and heptaglutamate conjugates are unstable under heat. Folic acid is also sensitive to copper and iron. Cobalamin is stable at mildly acidic pH, but it is rapidly destroyed by heat at alkaline pH, by light, or in the presence of trace metals (copper and iron, for example). Pyridoxine is stable to heat in acidic and alkaline solution, but it is light sensitive at neutral or alkaline pH. Pyridoxal, a major form of pyridoxine in milk and other foods, is heat labile.

In addition to the losses from chemical degradations stated above, all the water-soluble vitamins are susceptible to losses from leaching. The degree of loss depends on the solubility of the specific vitamin. Thus, thiamin, folic acid, ascorbic acid, pyridoxine, and niacin—which are all highly soluble in water—are easily lost through leaching, whereas the less soluble riboflavin is more resistant to leaching. Unlike water-soluble vitamins, fat-soluble vitamins (vitamin A; the carotenes, or provitamin A; vitamin D; vitamin E; and vitamin K) are stable against leaching losses but are susceptible to oxidative degradation, especially in the presence of light, metals, and other catalysts. Vitamin A and the carotenes are also heat labile because of their transformation into less active forms.

MINERALS. In general, processing has minor effects on minerals (for example, calcium, phosphorus, iron, and magnesium) in foods, except that losses from leaching can occur. Losses of trace minerals may occur, but the nutritional effects of this are less known.

EFFECTS OF RICE MILLING. The example of milled rice (see "Qualitative Requirements," above; see also chapter 2, the subsection "Product design") illustrates how alternative technologies can alter nutrient value. Rice is the basic food for more than half the world's population, and it supplies 70–80 percent of dietary caloric intake in the Orient. Rice in its hull is called rough rice or paddy rice. White rice is the polished endosperm that remains when other parts of the grain have been removed.

In rice milling a series of mechanical operations remove the hull, the embryo, and the outer layers of the rice kernel. When hulled brown rice is again passed through hullers or pearling cones, the

Table 4-3. *Approximate Composition of Selected Rice Products*
(percent)

Biological profile	Product				
	Brown rice	Polished rice	Parboiled rice	Bran	Polish
Protein	10.1	7.2–9.0	7.4	10.6–14.0	12.1–14.2
Carbohydrate	86.6	90.8	81.3	n.a.	59.9
Fat	2.4	0.34	0.3	11.7	12.7
Fiber	0.9	0.1	0.2	11.1	n.a.
Ash (minerals)	1.2	0.5	0.7	13.1	12.3

n.a., Not applicable.
Note: Percentages are calculated to a moisture-free basis.
Source: A. M. Altschul and R. W. Planck, "Effects of Commercial Processing of Cereals on Nutrient Content: Rice and Rice Products," in *Nutritional Evaluation of Food Processing*, 1st ed., ed. R. S. Harris and H. von Boesecke (New York: John Wiley and Sons, 1960), p. 204.

pericarp, most of the embryo, and the outer alenrone layers are removed as a powder called "bran." The inner alenrone layers and the remainder of the embryo are subsequently rubbed off by brushes, forming a powder called "polish." Bran is not used for human consumption and polish has limited uses because it tends to turn rancid quickly.[16] In the United States, for example, 8.5 percent of the whole grain weight of rice is removed as bran, and 1.8 percent is removed as polish.

The approximate composition of selected rice products is contained in table 4-3; vitamin content is shown in table 4-4. The percentages given in the tables indicate that those parts of the rice grain that are removed by milling—namely, the bran and the polish—are richer in nutrients than the endosperm. (The same, incidentally, is true of wheat.) Although whole rice is a good source of vitamins and minerals, these micronutrients are largely removed during milling. Although protein losses through milling are relatively small, protein fractions—which are rich in lysine, the first limiting amino acid in rice protein—are removed with the bran and polish. Thus, proteins in polished rice contain approximately

16. A. M. Altschul and R. W. Planck, "Effects of Commercial Processing of Cereal on Nutrient Content: Rice and Rice Products," in *Nutritional Evaluation of Food Processing*, 1st ed., ed. R. S. Harris and H. von Boesecke (New York: John Wiley and Sons, 1960), p. 204.

Table 4-4. *Vitamin Content of Selected Rice Products*
(milligrams in 100 grams)

	Product				
Vitamin	Brown rice	Polished rice	Parboiled rice	Bran	Polish
Biotin	0.12	0.04– 0.06	0.1	0.6	0.6
Folic acid	—	0.16	0.19	1.5	1.9
Niacin	46.2–47.2	10.0 –25.0	30.0–48.0	336.0	330.0
Pantothenic acid	10.3–17.0	6.4 – 8.0	13.7	22.0–27.7	33.3
Riboflavin	0.6	0.15– 0.31	0.3– 0.6	2.0	2.2
Thiamin	2.0– 4.8	0.4 – 0.8	1.9– 3.1	24.0	22.0
Vitamin B-6	6.9–10.3	3.3 – 4.5	—	25.0	20.0

—, Not available.
Source: Same as for table 4-3.

3.3 percent lysine,[17] whereas proteins in brown rice contain 4.5 percent lysine.[18] Estimates of nutrient retention in rice products, calculated from the data in tables 4-3 and 4-4, are given in table 4-5.

Although the degree of rice milling may be varied to increase nutrient retention, programs for promoting consumption of undermilled rice in undernourished populations are generally unsuccessful because of consumer prejudice against nonwhite rice. Undermilled rice, produced by hand milling with mortar and pestle or by limiting machine milling, is nutritionally superior to white, completely mechanically milled rice. Undermilled rice, however, is more apt to become rancid because of its high fat content; it is also susceptible to microbial damage because of its protein-rich outer layers. In some countries, rice is coated with glucose to 0.2 percent of its weight and with talc to 0.08 percent of its weight to increase the shininess of the grain.[19] This practice is nutritionally unsound because the asbestos in talc may be carcinogenic and because the rice has to be washed before it can be cooked, and washing causes further nutritional losses.

17. M. C. Kik, *Arkansas Agricultural Experimental Station Bulletin* (1957), p. 589; C. M. Lyman and others, *Journal of Agricultural Food Chemistry*, vol. 4 (1956), p. 1008.

18. C. H. Edwards and others, *Journal of Agricultural Food Chemistry*, vol. 3 (1955), p. 953.

19. Altschul and Planck, "Effects of Commercial Processing of Cereal," p. 204.

Table 4-5. *Estimated Nutrient Retention
in Selected Rice Products*
(percent)

| | Product | | | |
	Polished rice	Parboiled rice	Bran	Polish
Nutrient				
Protein	72	76	10	2
Carbohydrate	94	95	n.a.	1
Fat	13	13	42	10
Fiber	10	20	90	n.a.
Vitamins				
Biotin	37	75	32	9
Niacin	34	75	61	10
Pantothenic acid	48	91	16	5
Riboflavin	34	67	28	7
Thiamin	16	66	60	12
Vitamin B-6	41	—	25	4
Ash (minerals)	37	52	60	n.a.

n.a., Not applicable; —, not available.
Note: Estimates are based on the data given in tables 4-3 and 4-4 and are
derived by the following formulas:

$$\begin{array}{c} \text{percent} \\ \text{nutrient} \\ \text{loss} \end{array} = \frac{\left[\begin{array}{c} \text{percent} \\ \text{nutrient in} \\ \text{brown rice} \end{array} - \begin{array}{c} \text{percent} \\ \text{nutrient} \\ \text{in product} \end{array}\right] \times \dfrac{\begin{array}{c}\text{percent yield of}\\\text{product}\end{array}}{100 \text{ percent}}}{\text{percent nutrient in brown rice}};$$

percent nutrient retention = 100 percent — percent nutrient loss.

Percentage yield of product is assumed to be 8.5 percent for bran, 1.8 percent
for polish, 89.7 percent for polished rice, and 90 percent for parboiled rice.
Percentage nutrient retention in polished rice, bran, and polish does not always
add up to 100 percent because the data in tables 4-3 and 4-4 were originally
compiled by Altschul and Planck using data from various sources. When a
lower and an upper figure were given for nutrient content, the average of the
two numbers was used for calculations.
Source: Adapted from Altschul and Planck, "Effects of Commercial Processing on Cereals," p. 204.

It is clear from tables 4-4 and 4-5 that parboiled rice, which is
widely consumed in South Asia, retains most of the nutrients originally present in whole rice grain. In preparing parboiled rice,
rough rice is steeped in water, steamed, and dried in the sun before
milling. During this process, water-soluble nutrients in the germ
and alenrone layers are forced into the starchy endosperm of the
grain. The brief steaming gelatinizes the starch in the outer layer
of the endosperm and helps the polished rice retain the water-

soluble nutrients. Because of these effects, parboiling is a process that enhances a rice product's nutritional value.

EFFECTS OF WHEAT MILLING. Other grains than rice can be similarly affected by milling. From table 4-6 it is evident that the vitamin and mineral content of wheat products decreases markedly with milling until 70 percent extraction. These data indicate that wheat endosperm is a poor source of vitamins and minerals because most of these nutrients are concentrated in the germ and bran and are lost during milling. The decrease in the mineral content of wheat through milling is also important for quality control in the flour-milling industry, because high mineral content in flour is generally an indication of contamination by bran particles. Since phytate phosphorous (which complexes calcium and magnesium to form biologically unavailable salts) is removed faster than calcium in milling, calcium in flour is more biologically available than in whole wheat. Although only a small fraction of protein is removed

Table 4-6. *Estimated Nutrient Retention in Wheat Flour*
(percent)

Nutrient	Percentage nutrient retention by degree of whole wheat extraction in flour		
	High extraction (85 percent)	Standard extraction (70 percent)	Patent extraction (44 percent)
Protein	83	63	39
Carbohydrate	91	77	51
Fat	58	35	15
Fiber	47	3	...
Vitamins			
Niacin	19	10	5
Riboflavin	54	24	13
Thiamin	70	17	5
Vitamin B-6	n.d.	10	4
Vitamin E	n.d.	8	2
Ash (minerals)	41	18	10

n.d., Not detected; ..., retained in trace amounts.
Note: Estimates are derived by the following formulas:

$$\text{percent nutrient loss} = \frac{\left[\begin{array}{c}\text{percent nutrient in whole wheat}\end{array} - \begin{array}{c}\text{percent nutrient in product}\end{array}\right] \times \dfrac{\text{percent extraction}}{100 \text{ percent}} \times \dfrac{\text{percent relative nutrient concentration}}{100 \text{ percent}}}{\text{percent nutrient in whole wheat}};$$

percent nutrient retention = 100 percent − percent nutrient loss.

with the wheat germ and bran, milling decreases lysine and trypto-phan content because bran protein is richer in lysine and trypto-phan than endosperm protein. (Even before the bran and germ are removed, wheat protein is low in lysine and tryptophan relative to other grains.) Milling also decreases the fat content of wheat prod-ucts; such decrease reduces the caloric value per unit of the wheat product but increases the storage stability of the products against their becoming rancid. British firms have used higher extraction rates for wheat (80–85 percent) with minimal change in the color of the flour and the baking quality.[20]

EFFECTS OF FRUIT AND VEGETABLE PROCESSING. Fruits and vegetables can also suffer significant losses of micronutrients during process-ing. The losses vary with crop, nutrient, and process. For example, the steam blanching of peas causes a 12.3 percent loss of their vi-tamin C content, whereas water blanching causes a 25.8 percent loss.[21] Some nutrients can be almost totally lost during canning; canned corn, for instance, loses 80 percent of its thiamin.[22]

PRODUCT FORTIFICATION AND MODIFICATION. When the process-ing firm's choice of technology significantly affects the nutritional quality of its product, the government or industrial associations usually intervene to regulate the decision. The agroindustrial ana-lyst should note such negative technological effects as nutrient losses and attempt to minimize them by adjusting the technology or by restoring nutrients through fortification. Food technology in this regard is not necessarily a nutritional liability; it can enhance nutritional value by fortifying the product against nutrient losses unavoidable in processing and by retarding spoilage or transform-ing poor nutrient resources into foods of higher value.[23] Nutritional transformation of this kind has been the work of the Institute of

20. R. J. Dimler, "Effects of Commercial Processing of Cereals on Nutrient Content: Milling, Part A: Wheat," in *Nutritional Evaluation of Food Process-ing*, 1st ed., pp. 197–204.

21. D. B. Lund, "Effects of Blanching, Pasteurization, and Sterilization on Nutrients," in *Nutritional Evaluation of Food Processing*, 2d ed. (1975), p. 205.

22. Ibid.

23. For a further discussion of fortification, see James E. Austin (ed.), *Global Malnutrition and Cereal Fortification* (Cambridge, Mass.: Ballinger Publish-ing Co., 1979); and *Confronting Urban Malnutrition*, pp. 71–75.

Food Product Research and Development in Thailand.[24] The institute focused its research on the protein residue of the mung bean, which was being extracted and discarded by Thai starch factories. Through food technology the institute created a protein isolate and transformed it by extrusion into a nutrient-dense weaning food for preschoolers. Thus, technology was employed to recapture a wasted by-product and transform it into a form suited to use by a nutritionally vulnerable group.[25]

Salient points for project analysis

The following questions summarize the major considerations the project analyst should examine in reviewing an agroindustrial project's selection of technology.

Is the processing technology consistent with the qualitative requirements of the marketplace?
• Match with qualitative standards of market segments?
• Incremental revenue versus added technological investment?
• Technology appropriate for local and export markets?

What constraints do process requirements impose?
• Nature of requirements?
• Number of technological options?
• Scale requirements?
• Demand adequate for scale?

Which technology has the lowest socioeconomic costs?
• Mixes of labor and capital?
• Raw material usage?

24. Nevin Scrimshaw and others, *High-Protein Product Development in Thailand*, Technical Report Series, no. 1 (Cambridge, Mass.: Massachusetts Institute of Technology, International Nutrition Planning Program, 1973).

25. For further discussion of the technological options and the potential and problems of nutritious formulated foods, see Jerianne Heimendinger, Marian Zeitlin, and James Austin, *Nutrition Intervention in Developing Countries: Formulated Foods*, U.S. Agency for International Development (USAID), Special Study no. 3 (Cambridge, Mass.: Oelgeschlager, Gunn, and Hain, 1980); and Alan Berg, "Industry's Struggle with Malnutrition," *Harvard Business Review*, vol. 50, no. 1 (January-February 1972), pp. 130–41.

- Energy requirements?
- Biomass-based energy sources?

How will the technology affect use of project capacity?
- Adjustments to diversify products processed and lengthen operating cycle?
- Costs and benefits of adjustments?

How well does the technology fit with the firm's managerial capability?
- Supervisory skills adequate?
- Technical skills adequate?
- Adjust technology to reduce skill requirements?

What are the technology's nutritional consequences?
- Effects on quality and quantity of nutrients?
- Methods of minimizing nutrient loss or increasing nutritional quality through adjusting technology?

Plant Location

In addition to technology selection, the location of the processing plant is another critical decision in project design. The first criterion for plant location is the relation between raw materials and markets, with transport an essential factor to be considered. Other considerations are labor supply, the availability of infrastructure, land costs, and developmental effect.

Raw materials, markets, and transport

The plant must decide whether to locate near the raw material or near the market for finished goods. The decision depends on the characteristics of the raw material and its transformative process, as well as on the costs and availability of transport services. Conditions of raw materials and transport that favor locating near raw material suppliers are:

- Highly perishable produce that requires immediate processing—for example, cucumbers, melons, or sugarcane;

- Fragile products that can sustain minimal handling—for example, eggs or tomatoes;
- Products that are considerably reduced in weight or volume by processing, thus facilitating transport—for example, lumber, grain, cotton, grapes, or sugarcane.

Conditions of raw materials and transport that favor locating near the market for finished goods are:

- Produce that is not very perishable or fragile—for example, potatoes;
- Products for which processing adds weight or volume—for example, bottled or canned beverages;
- Processing that requires supplies from different sources—for example, pencil manufacturing.

The decision on location requires the ranking of one factor, such as transport costs, against another.[26] As transport technologies change, costs shift and the economics of the plant's location can alter. In the United States, for example, declining costs for grain transport made it economical for flour mills to shift from distant grain collection points to urban centers, thus providing better service to nearby consumers. In contrast, meat packers in the United States have moved from cities to animal-producing areas, thereby saving on transport and processing costs.

Transport costs are also central to decisions regarding the number and size of the plants an agroindustry should construct. If raw material suppliers or markets are scattered and transport costs are high, it may be advisable for the firm to have multiple plants rather than one large plant. The savings on transport may offset the economies of scale from a single-plant operation.

The economic importance of transport will also be related to the value of the product. For example, a high-value produce for export, such as cut flowers, would have a relatively lower elasticity of demand for transport because transport costs are a small percentage of total costs. A firm processing such a product would be more

26. In general, trucks are more economical for short hauls, railroads for medium, and ships for long. Air transport is particularly appropriate for high-value products and for products for which speed is critical.

concerned with locating near the supplier—to lessen the risk of perishability—and with the quality of the transport service (for example, speed and refrigeration) than with transport costs. Transport services deficient in quality or availability may eliminate some desirable locations. When this occurs, the firm should consider integrating to operate its own transport services. Integration would require an analysis of the incremental capital investment and the potential savings in increased reliability.

Labor supply

Because agroindustries do not generally employ many workers, their supply of unskilled labor is not constrained, particularly if the workers from which the project draws are highly mobile. It is more difficult, however, to find skilled labor and managerial talent, a constraint especially acute if the plant is in a rural area. If this is the case, the firm may have to offer special financial incentives or social amenities to attract and retain qualified personnel.

Availability of infrastructure

Because defective infrastructure can increase costs and negatively affect quality, the agroindustrial firm should consider the facilities and services available at alternative locations. Puri and Lamson-Scribner have recommended that a firm examine a location for the following infrastructural aspects of electricity and water supply.[27]

Electricity
- Demand (both actual and projected, to identify possible bottlenecks): plant, community
- Source and availability
- Reliability
  Record of interruptions during past year (some utility companies do not regard momentary outage as an "interruption"; hence, verify the record)

27. G. N. Puri and Frank Lamson-Scribner, "Technical Aspects of Appraisal," EDI Report no. CN439 (Washington, D.C., World Bank, May 1976; processed); also see United Nations Industrial Development Organization (UNIDO), *Manual for the Preparation of Industrial Feasibility Studies*, Sales no. E.78.II.B.5 (New York, 1978), pp. 54–97; and S. Soderman, *Industrial Location Planning* (New York: Halsted, 1975).

- Availability of desired demand on year-round basis
- Tie-ins with state power grid
    Effect of grid outages on power for plant site
    Willingness of electricians to repair "hot" or live lines
- Cost of purchased power
    Terms of contract
    Documentation

Potable water
- Demand, load and pressures, temperatures
- Source and availability
- Boiler feed-water treatment required
- Cost
- Kind of boiler fuel, its source and availability

Cooling water
- Maximum wet bulb design
- Cooling tower; river water or seawater?
- Intake works
- Discharge
- Corrosion protection
- Pollution problem
- Distance to intake
- Right of way for supply and discharge
- Permits required
    Officials: names, titles, addresses
    Obtained by whom?
    When?
    Present status
    Documentation
- Cost

Process water
- Demand (both actual and projected) and load at full capacity
- Source and availability
- Treatment
- Cost

In addition, the analyst should also assess the transport infrastructure, including roads, railroad sidings, and storage terminals. In one East African country, a corned-beef processing plant was experiencing raw material shortages while at the same time cattle growers in a neighboring province were unable to bring their animals to the plant because the roads and climate were not suitable for transport of live animals. Consequently, the government helped the cattlemen put up a slaughterhouse and freezing plant in the cattle-raising areas. The frozen beef blocks were then transported to the corned-beef plant for further processing.

If the infrastructure is deficient, the project should compare the investment cost of its providing this infrastructure against the advantages of the location. Similarly, and even when there are sources of public power, the plant should consider incorporating an emergency generator to ensure against costly power outages.

The social infrastructure—including housing, schools, health, and recreational facilities—should also be inventoried because these social components may affect the project's ability to recruit the necessary personnel.

Social infrastructure should generally be established with the cooperation of the government and should incorporate community ownership of facilities. This sharing of responsibilities minimizes the managerial and social problems associated with "company towns."

Some governments have promoted agroindustries by creating industrial estates or parks. These developments provide the production infrastructure for a complex of agroindustries, encourage complementary industries to locate together, and permit greater efficiency by the firms' sharing services (buying or marketing) and facilities. In rural areas, however, they have sometimes created "islands" of developmental activity that are not integrated into and do not affect the adjoining rural areas.

Land costs

Land costs usually represent a relatively small percentage of total capital outlay because processing plants are not land extensive. Nonetheless, land costs vary, and comparative shopping for a site is necessary. If the owner of the project's potential land is also a project promoter, the land cost should be compared with other land costs to verify its fair market value. Urban land is usually more expensive than rural land, but the price depends on the site's alternative uses. The firm should purchase enough land to accommodate future expansion. Suburban expansion increases land values and the cost of future land acquisitions. Locating in cities experiencing rapid urbanization may also result in subsequent traffic congestion and higher transport costs.

Developmental effects

One final consideration on a plant's location concerns the different developmental effects of alternative locations. The analyst should consider the increased employment and income redistribution the project will generate. Developing relatively backward regions may be a governmental priority, and the locating of a processing plant in a backward region might provide the necessary market outlet to stimulate agricultural production, furnish a use for marginal lands, or stem rural-to-urban migration. Bates, for example, found rural prosperity and rural emigration to be inversely related.[28] Although not an optimal location, a site may be selected because it fulfills a country's sociopolitical objectives.[29] A government may provide fiscal incentives to compensate firms for the added costs of locating in underdeveloped regions in support of its development policies. These benefits may make a project's financial return compatible with its economic return, thus ensuring the project's implementation.

Salient points for project analysis

The analyst should consider the following questions in deciding where to locate the agroindustrial plant.

Do raw material, market, and transport factors support the proposed location?
- Perishability of the raw material?
- Reduction or increase in product's weight or volume?
- Cost and quality of transport services?
- Multiple plants versus single plant?
- Should plant provide own transport?

28. Robert Bates, *Rural Responses to Industrialization* (New Haven: Yale University Press, 1976), p. 252.
29. United Nations, *Industrial Location and Regional Development*, Proceedings of Interregional Seminar, August 1968, Sales no. 71.II.B.18 (New York, 1971).

Is there an adequate labor supply?
• Unskilled, skilled, managerial supply adequate?
• Special personnel incentives required?

Is the infrastructure at the location acceptable?
• Energy and water supply, their ecological effects, reliability, and cost?
• Fire protection facilities?
• Transport?
• Social infrastructure?

What will be the plant's land cost?
• Comparative prices for a square meter?
• Adequate to future needs?

What will be the developmental effects of the location?
• On employment and income distribution?
• On regional development?
• Fiscal incentives for plant to support development?

Inventory Management

Inventory management for agroindustries is complicated by the biological nature and the seasonality of the raw material. The analyst should particularly examine the capacity factors, physical facilities, and financial aspects of the project.

Storage capacity

The purpose of managing raw material inventory is to minimize the disequilibrium between supply and processing capacity. Seasonal raw materials may require the plant to store, at one time, its entire annual or semiannual input requirements. Some raw materials, however, must be quickly processed because of their high perishability. When this occurs, the need to store the raw material is greatly reduced, and the capacity for processing and the production of finished goods are increased.

Processing reduces some products' ability to be stored, and a plant's failure to anticipate this change can cause significant problems for inventory management. For example, a wheat flour processor in the Philippines constructed minimal wheat storage but built and rented considerable space for storing finished flour.[30] When demand fell, the company possessed large inventories of perishable flour that, even with chemical treatment, had a shelf life of only four months. Under proper conditions, wheat can be stored for years, but after processing it is much more perishable. The problem was exacerbated by a large grain shipment that arrived and, because of the lack of silos, had to be immediately processed.

One alternative for plant inventory management is intermediate storage. The raw material can be semiprocessed—into forms such as tomato paste, orange juice concentrate, or powdered milk, for example—to reduce its perishability and then can be inventoried for subsequent processing. Semiprocessing offers the advantage of reducing the plant's investment in finishing equipment and permits the plant to work a longer period, thereby reducing the costs of idle capacity.

The analyst should consider the tradeoff between the costs of raw material and inventory facilities for finished goods. If the size of the raw material is significantly reduced in processing—for example, oranges converted into frozen juice—the space requirements for the inventory of finished goods will be substantially lower. The quality and cost of the storage facilities may differ, however; in the example of frozen orange juice, the difference is between nonrefrigerated and refrigerated storage. In any event, the perishability and seasonality of agroindustrial raw materials require that standard inventory management procedures—for example, economic order quantity systems—be altered.[31] The plant should also ensure that there is adequate inventory capacity for supplies and processing inputs other than raw material, including parts for equipment repair. These inventories generally require minimal cost and space,

30. Edward Felton and Ralph Sorenson, "Republic Flour Mills, Inc.," Case Study no. ICH 12M30 (Manila: Inter-University Program for Graduate Business Education, 1966).

31. For a description of some of these procedures, see J. Orlicky, *Material Requirements Planning* (New York: McGraw-Hill, 1975); O. W. Wright, *Production and Inventory Management in the Computer Age* (Boston: Cahny Books, 1974); and D. C. Whybark and J. G. Williams, "Material Requirements Planning under Uncertainty," *Decision Sciences*, vol. 7, no. 4 (October 1976), pp. 595–606.

but not having them on hand can bring an entire processing operation to a halt.

Physical facilities

Food losses after harvest have been estimated at 10–30 percent.[32] The major causes of losses are pest and insect infestation and microbial infiltration.[33] Proper storage can partially eliminate these causes (see chapter 3, the subsections "Competing uses of raw material. Losses" and "Determinants of Quality. Handling and transport; Storage"). Inventory facilities should include preparation facilities, such as drying houses, as well as storage structures. The storability of, and appropriate storage facilities for, cereals, legumes, animal products, fruits, and vegetables are discussed below.

CEREALS. Grains contain more than 20 percent moisture at harvest and are highly susceptible to deterioration from microbial growth and pest and insect damage. Cereal grains (seeds consisting of a seed coat and an embryo of reserve nutrients) are resistant to deterioration when they are dried to a moisture content below 14–15 percent. Drying treatments increase the storage stability of unmilled grains because, at moisture levels of about 14–15 percent or above, microbial growth may create "hot spots" (localized areas of temperature increase) that can char the stored grains. Grains that are improperly dried in a field can develop mold and musty odors. Even in the United States, with its developed agroindustrial technology, losses in stored grain from insects, pests, and microorganisms were estimated to be as high as 9 percent of the total crop in 1974.[34] If its storage of unmilled cereal grain is in bins, storage huts, and bags, a plant can minimize adverse changes in the grain's nutritional value and taste by ventilating the supply to prevent the moisture from condensing and by protecting the supply from insects and rodents. At moisture levels below 14–

32. E. A. Asselbergs, "FAO Action Programme for the Prevention of Food Losses," speech delivered to the Agribusiness Management for the Developed and Developing World Food System Seminar (Boston: Harvard University, Graduate School of Business Administration, May 31, 1978).

33. E. R. Pariser and others, *Post-Harvest Food Losses in Developing Countries* (Washington, D.C.: National Academy of Sciences), pp. 47–109.

34. Robert M. May, "Food Lost to Pests," *Nature*, vol. 267 (June 23, 1977).

15 percent, there is very little change in the proteins, carbohydrates, fats, vitamins, and minerals in cereal grains.

In addition to its causing losses in the nutrients and organoleptic qualities of grains, microbial growth can also produce toxic metabolites that, if consumed, may be hazardous to a person's health. Grain that has been damaged during storage by fermentation, insect and pest infestation, microbial respiration ("hot spots"), or sprouting is often mixed with sound grain to produce a mixture that is organoleptically acceptable for human consumption. This is, however, a dangerous practice because of the microbial toxins that storage-damaged grains may contain, toxins that are not easily destroyed by processing. Damaged grain of this kind also has inferior nutritional and sanitary qualities. Feeding damaged grains to livestock is similarly dangerous because the animals may die of the microbial toxins or the toxins may affect certain tissues that are later consumed by humans. Damaged grain can be used to produce commercial alcohol. The process involves a distillation step that removes microbial toxins, and the ethanol yield from damaged grain is comparable to that of sound grain (unless there has been extensive carbohydrate degradation).[35] Some nations have mixed grain alcohol with gasoline to make "gasohol," an alternative fuel (Brazil is making heavy investments to produce alcohol from sugarcane and cassava for this purpose).[36]

Milled grain products are less stable to insect and pest infestation, microbial growth, and chemical degradation than unmilled whole grains because milling removes the grain's protective seed coat. Nevertheless, storage as for unmilled whole grains—in dry and cool conditions—will result in minimal nutrient changes and good palatability in milled products. One danger is that the fat in milled products may chemically oxidize and become rancid. Whole wheat flour, brown rice, and whole corn have shelf lives of only a few weeks or months because they quickly become rancid.[37]

35. L. Zeleny, "Effects of Commercial Storage on the Nutrient Content of Processed Foods: Cereal Grains," and A. M. Altschul and R. W. Planck, "Effects of Commercial Processing of Cereals on Nutrient Content: Rice and Rice Products," both in *Nutritional Evaluation of Food Processing*, 1st ed., pp. 353 and 204, respectively.

36. World Bank, "Alcohol Production from Biomass."

37. Zeleny, "Effects of Commercial Storage," p. 353.

LEGUMES. Storage of oil-rich seeds also requires their drying to avoid deterioration; best conditions for drying are to a moisture level of approximately 7 percent.[38] Because the moisture level in stored seeds depends primarily on atmospheric moisture, leguminous seeds stored in humid, tropical, or subtropical regions may deteriorate from mold growth and the release of free fatty acids. Mold causes a loss of organoleptic quality (for example, off-flavor in cooked beans) and aids the potential formation of toxic compounds (mycotoxins). When the seed accumulates free fatty acids, it has a lower yield of edible oil and a lower "smoke point" to its crude oil (the smoke point is the temperature at which oil becomes smoky). For instance, the free fatty acid content of cottonseeds increases from 4.3 percent to 30 percent when cottonseed containing 11.9 percent moisture is stored in bins for ten days.[39] Stored leguminous seeds deteriorate more quickly with a high moisture level when a large percentage of already damaged seeds are present.[40]

MEAT PRODUCTS. Fresh meat products are susceptible to rapid spoilage from both microbial growth and enzyme action. The organoleptic quality of fresh meat is so perishable that there are probably no significant nutrient losses before spoilage makes the product unacceptable for consumption. Meat must be refrigerated to prevent deterioration. Stored processed meats, however, do not lose significant nutrients unless they are stored in high temperatures with a high water content.

FRUITS AND VEGETABLES. Although fruits and vegetables usually contain few proteins, they are the major source of vitamin C. Several fruits and vegetables (for example, apricots, peaches, melons, cherries, carrots, leafy green vegetables, and sweet potatoes) also are sources of provitamin-A carotenes. Thus, the most relevant data on nutrient retention in fruits and vegetables concern vitamins C

38. V. L. Frampton, "Effect of Commercial Processing of Oilseeds and Oils on Their Composition; Part A: Effect of Processing on Composition of Oilseeds," in *Nutritional Evaluation of Food Processing*, 1st ed., p. 238.

39. A. M. Altschul and others, *Oil and Soap*, vol. 20 (1943), p. 258.

40. A. M. Altschul, *Cottonseed and Cottonseed Products*, ed. A. E. Baily (New York: Interscience Publishers, 1948).

and A. The sizable losses of these nutrients through storage—and their significant preservation through adequate refrigerated storage—are shown in table 4-7. In assessing the inventory facilities' requirements, the analyst should compare the potential physical and qualitative losses with the investment outlay needed to minimize them.

The final aspect of the analysis is the location of the inventory facilities. As noted in the chapters on marketing and procurement, it may be desirable to locate the warehouses near producers to facilitate assembling economical lots or near distributors to provide rapid delivery service. The firm may decide to have separate warehouses to reduce the risk of fire losses (an important consideration, for example, in baled cotton warehousing) and thereby reduce insurance premiums. The earlier example of the Indian apple project (see "Qualitative requirements," above) illustrates the importance of storage location. The field heat of apples must be reduced within 24 hours of picking to extend their shelf life and nutritional qualities. Therefore, apple firms should locate their storage centers near the production areas. Such location also allows the firm to transport the apples to the processing centers in nonrefrigerated trucks, thereby saving on this added investment cost.

Financial aspects

The seasonal nature of agroindustrial products raises the peak working capital requirements of agroindustries to levels higher than those of other processing operations. Many processors have encountered problems of capitalization because of inaccurately estimated needs for working capital. Thus, the analyst should ascertain the periods of peak working capital needs and verify that credit lines correspond to these peaks. Another financial determinant is the price level of the raw material. This will only be known at harvest time unless a fixed price, long-term contract exists. Consequently, credit lines must be flexible enough to cover price variations.

Large inventories also increase the processor's price risk. The price of the processed product can fall during the inventory period, thus leaving the processor with fixed raw material costs and a lower profit margin. Many U.S. processors use the futures markets (for

Table 4-7. *Losses of Vitamins C and A in Selected Vegetables under Various Storage Conditions*

Vegetable	Storage condition	Loss (percent)
	Vitamin C	
Asparagus	24 hours at 19–25°C	20–40
	24 hours at 2°C	3
	1 week at 0°C	50
	1 week at 21°C	70
Broccoli	24 hours at 21°C	50
	24 hours at 8–10°C	10–30
	96 hours at 21°C	80
	96 hours at 8–10°C	25–40
Green beans	24 hours at 21°C	20
	24 hours at 8–10°C	10
	96 hours at 21°C	30
Kale	3 weeks at 0°C	40
	2 days at 21°C	40
	9 days at 0°C[a]	40
	1 day at 21°C[a]	40
Snap beans	10 days at 0°C	40
	6 days at 10°C	40
Spinach	24 hours at 21°C	34–48
	48 hours at 21°C	78
	192 hours at 21°C	95
	72 hours at 1–3°C	0
Swiss chard	24 hours at 21°C	35
	96 hours at 21°C	85
	24 hours at 8–10°C	30
	96 hours at 8–10°C	70
	Vitamin A	
Carrots	1 month at 21°C	Slight
Collards	4 days at 0°C	2
	4 days at 21°C[a]	82
Kale	4 days at 0°C	0
	4 days at 21°C[a]	76
Peas	48 hours at 21°C	15–27
Spinach	37 hours at 21°C	Slight
Swiss chard	24 hours at 21°C	0

°C, degrees Celsius.
Source: J. M. Krochta and B. Feinberg, "Effects of Harvesting and Handling on the Composition of Fruits and Vegetables," in *Nutritional Evaluation of Food Processing*, 2d ed., p. 98; H. W. von Boesecke, "Effects of Harvesting and Handling Practices on Composition of Unprocessed Foods: Foods of Plant Origin," in *Nutritional Evaluation of Food Processing*, 1st ed., p. 58.
a. Wilting occurs under these conditions.

example, in grains, orange juice, livestock, potatoes) to hedge against the inventory price risk.[41] Although there are budding futures markets in some developing countries, most of the developing world lacks the conditions for futures markets (standardized product grades, ability to deliver, highly developed information systems, and large pools of speculative capital). Commodity exporters in the developing nations can, however, use the futures markets of the industrialized nations to obtain some price protection for their exports.

There are alternative approaches to price management. If the processor buys from wholesalers and the product does not have to be processed as soon as it is harvested, the processor can buy the product as it is needed and minimize inventories. The tradeoff is that, to save inventory carrying costs and the investment in physical facilities and to reduce price risk, the processor may have to pay the distributor premium prices for providing these services and carrying the risk. If the harvest is short, inadequate storage facilities for stocking up at harvest time can leave a processor with product shortages, production stoppage later, or with high prices from the wholesaler. If the processor does carry the inventory, it may use forward contracts as a surrogate for the futures market: the factory's expected output would be sold in advance at a fixed price expected to cover costs and preserve a margin. A fixed price might be favored by retailers or further processors because it is stable. Both seller and buyer reduce their uncertainty, although the buyer still carries the end-market price risks.

Salient points for project analysis

In examining the project's inventory management, the analyst should consider the following questions.

What will be the best storage capacities for raw materials and finished goods?
- Product perishability?
- Effect of processing on storability?

41. Henry Arthur, *Commodity Futures as a Business Management Tool* (Boston: Harvard University, Graduate School of Business Administration, Division of Research, 1971).

- Raw versus semi-processed material to reduce storage needed for finished goods?
- Storage for processing supplies and repair parts?

Are the facilities adequate?
- Costs and benefits of reducing inventory deterioration?
- Location relative to producers and distributors?

Have the requirements for working capital and the inventory price risks been adequately analyzed?
- Peak needs for working capital?
- Feasible to hedge price risks through futures markets?
- Continued buying versus stockpiling?
- Advance contracting?

Supplies for Processing

Although the dominant input for the processing operation is the agricultural raw material,[42] there are other supplies that also deserve the analyst's attention. The analyst should determine whether adequate quantities and qualities of these ancillary supplies will be available when needed and at a reasonable cost. Source alternatives and nutritional value should also be examined. Selected references on industrial procurement, including a listing of UNIDO guides to information sources on a variety of agroindustries, are provided in the fourth section of the bibliography.

Alternative sources

The major ancillary agroindustrial supplies are packaging materials, added ingredients (for example, flavorings and preservatives), processing chemicals, as well as maintenance supplies. Local sources are preferable but frequently not feasible. The manufacturing of the aforementioned ancillary supplies is a secondary industry that operates on derived demand. Consequently, the development of these various kinds of supplies is usually slower than that of the

42. Although this is true of most agroindustries, some, such as textiles, have become increasingly dependent on synthetic rather than natural raw materials.

primary industry. Where local manufacturers of ancillary supplies exist, the quality of their inputs may not adequately meet the requirements of export or even domestic markets. This is particularly true for packaging supplies because product preservation and appearance can be important variables in the consumer's purchasing process. Maintenance supplies—for example, spare parts—may not be produced locally because of low demand.

The processor may be forced to rely on imported ancillary supplies until these local industries are established or improved. The processor can stimulate their industrial development through contracts, technical assistance, and supervision planned for their improvement. Alternatively, the processor can integrate and begin producing these inputs. Integration is more feasible when the processor's input needs are great or the production technology for the input is adaptable to small-scale production (for example, crates produced with a sawmill). The disadvantages of relying on imports are the foreign exchange requirements, delivery delays, high transport costs, and import duties.

Nutritional considerations

The quality of ancillary supplies for packaging is especially important because packaging can affect a product's nutritional value. Poor packaging, especially in tropical climates, can cause spoilage, a shorter shelf life, and nutritional deterioration in a product. For example, canning protects products from insects, microbes, and other agents of deterioration (such as sunlight), but if it is done improperly it can cause botulism, an acute food poisoning potentially fatal to humans. Yet materials that are needed to preserve product quality can significantly increase product costs (and can sometimes even remove a product from the reach of low-income consumers), so that analysts must make the best possible compromise between adequate packaging and nutritional needs. The processor should also be sensitive to the possibly adverse nutritional effects of certain preservatives and coloring or flavoring agents. Such added ingredients should be reviewed to see if they meet international safety standards.

Salient points for project analysis

To examine supplies for processing, the analyst should consider the following questions.

Where should the plant procure its ancillary supplies (packaging, ingredients, and chemicals)?
- Locally or abroad?
- Foreign exchange requirements if purchased abroad?
- Development of local suppliers?
- Horizontal integration?

What are the nutritional effects of the ancillary materials?
- Nutrient retention?
- Effects of packaging on price and consumption by low-income groups?

Programming and Control

There are two aspects of programming and control that particularly merit the agroindustrial project analyst's attention: production design and quality control.

Production design

The analyst should review at least the following items of the project's production design: its implementation plans, engineering, and production scheduling.[43]

IMPLEMENTATION PLANS. The focus of this book has been on the analysis and design phase of the project cycle (see chapter 1, the subsection "Three components of the analytical framework"), but, even in this context, it is important for the analyst to ensure that the investment, if approved, can be successfully implemented. Consequently, a preliminary implementation plan should exist that delineates the steps to be taken after the investment decision and before production begins.

To guide this phase the project can make use of such management techniques as Gantt charts, which divide the implementation process into distinct activities with time periods attached to each.

43. These elements are also important for ssi's and will frequently require external assistance. The UNIDO Expert Group has cited such assistance as critical to ssi success: UNIDO, *Industrialization and Rural Development* (New York, 1978), pp. 9–16.

For more complex projects, other network diagramming techniques —such as the Critical Path Method (cpm) or Project Evaluation and Review Technique (pert)—might be used.[44] In formulating or reviewing the implementation schedule, the analyst should keep in mind the seasonal nature of the agroindustry's raw material. The timing of this availability sets basic temporal parameters for the start of production.

PROJECT ENGINEERING. The project's investments, production design, and organization should be based on detailed engineering, the degree and sophistication of which will depend on the size and nature of the undertaking. UNIDO has indicated the following charts and layouts as typically useful:[45]

- *General functional layouts.* These show the relations among equipment, buildings, and civil works.
- *Materials flow diagrams.* Such charts show the direction and quantities of all inputs (for example, materials, supplies, and utilities) and outputs (for example, intermediate and final products, by-products, and emissions) throughout the plant; for agroindustries it is useful to extend these diagrams back through raw material procurement, especially if the product is highly perishable and may require special preprocessing treatment.
- *Production-line diagrams.* These show the location, equipment specifications, space requirements, utilities requirements, and mounting device sizes for each processing stage.
- *Transport layouts.* These diagrams show the distances and modes of transport inputs and outputs to, within, and from the production line.
- *Utility consumption layouts.* These show the location and quantity of utility requirements for the purpose of guiding installation and calculating costs.

---

44. See United Nations, *Programming and Control of Implementation of Industrial Projects in Developing Countries,* ID/SER.L/1, Sales no. 70.II.B.18; and *The Initiation and Implementation of Industrial Projects in Developing Countries: A Systematic Approach,* ID/146, Sales no. 75.II.B.2 (New York, 1970 and 1975, respectively).

45. UNIDO, *Manual for the Preparation of Industrial Feasibility Studies,* pp. 108–09.

- *Communications layouts.* These diagrams show the location and kind of communications device needed throughout the facility.
- *Manpower layouts.* These indicate the number and skill level of personnel needed at each stage of the production process and are useful in identifying areas in which labor intensity can be increased.
- *Physical layouts.* These charts fit the functional layouts to the actual conditions at the site and are thus based on geodetic, geological, hydrological, soil, mechanical, and other surveys.[46]

PRODUCTION SCHEDULING. Production scheduling needs to be examined because it is complicated by the raw material's seasonality. The processor should design a master schedule that programs dates and quantities of raw material procurement, processing volume and duration, and inventory levels. From this the analyst can explore the possibilities of reducing investment in equipment capacity by operating multiple shifts, extending the processing period by multiple crop inputs or semiprocessing of raw materials, minimizing fluctuations in product flow, and attaining adequate quantities of labor and supplies. For example, the production schedule of a milk-processing plant might show a strong seasonal variation in capacity use because of the drop in milk production from the lack of cattle forage in a dry season. This variation might stimulate the processor to use soy for protein feed in the off-season and to produce soy-based milk as another of its products to maintain output. In effect, the production schedule becomes the working document for analyzing many of the issues examined in the previous sections.

Quality control

Developing countries' agroindustries frequently lack systematic quality-control procedures. As a result, their product quality is erratic, can cause consumer dissatisfaction, and, sometimes, can be hazardous for consumption.

Product quality is influenced by many factors, beginning with the genetic material (seed or breed) used on the farm and with the

---

46. Also see Economic Development Foundation, *Manual on Plant Layout and Material Handling* (Tokyo: Asian Productivity Organization, 1971); and Siegmar Frey, *Plant Layout* (Munich: Hansen, 1975).

farmer's agricultural practices. As discussed in chapter 3 (the section "Acceptable Quality"), quality control must begin at the stage of raw material production. At the processing stage, quality control should be applied to the raw material inventory, work in process, and finished goods. The quality of the raw material stock can be preserved by adequate storage facilities (see the section on inventory management, above), but periodic sampling of the inventory to test for pest or insect damage or microbial growth is advisable. These measures can spot problems in time for the plant's management to take corrective measures. Spoilage can begin inconspicuously and accelerate rapidly, causing massive inventory losses and production stoppages. By contrast, monitoring is relatively inexpensive and, usually, cost effective.

Most food and fiber processing is relatively quick, but in-process monitoring is feasible for such aspects as contamination levels, packaging integrity, temperature, and chemical composition. Finished goods can be inspected by variable (that is, a particular characteristic) or by attribute (to sort good from bad). Quality-control mechanisms include visual inspection, mechanical measuring devices, and laboratory analyses. Sampling techniques are relatively reliable and efficient, but the processor must first set an acceptable level of quality. After acceptable quality is defined, sampling can take place within limits of probability for committing either a "Type I" error (accepting a lot that should be rejected) or a "Type II" error (rejecting a lot that should be accepted). Nutritional quality of finished goods should be monitored by biochemical analysis to measure nutrient retention and any microbial contamination.

Salient points for project analysis

To examine programming and quality control, the analyst should consider the following questions.

Is there a clear and systematic implementation plan?
• Postinvestment and preproduction steps delineated?
• Programming techniques such as Gantt charts, CPM, or PERT used?

Has project engineering been carried out diagrammatically?
• General functional layouts made?
• Flow diagrams of materials designed?

- Production-line diagrams specified?
- Transport, utility, communications, and manpower layouts set forth?

Does a master schedule for procurement and processing exist?
- Seasonal availability of raw material considered?
- Possibility of working multiple shifts?
- Alternative uses of production capacity?

Are there systematic quality-control procedures for raw materials, work in process, and finished goods?
- Inspection system for raw material as it is grown?
- Controls for contamination levels, packaging integrity, temperature, and chemical composition?
- Sampling procedures? laboratory testing facilities?
- Nutritional quality verifiable?
- Corrective procedures specified?

By-products

One final aspect of processing is the role of by-products. Unlike other manufacturing operations, agroindustrial processing generally disaggregates one raw material, rather than aggregating various materials. The biological nature of the raw material allows it to have many useful parts, and the product often has multiple derivatives. Because by-products can be important in the economics of agroindustries, they warrant close inspection.

Economic value

The analyst should identify all the outputs of the processing flow because almost all have a realizable economic value. Pure wastage should be minimized, but economic opportunities from possible by-products are often overlooked, especially in an agroindustry's early development. The analyst should look for recoverable but economically unexploited by-products. Such an example (cited earlier under "Selection of Processing Technology. Nutritional consequences.") is discarded mung bean protein used as weaning food or animal feed. An example of a neglected by-product can be seen in the case of broiler chicken processors in Guyana who initially failed to retain the discarded chicken blood for use as a protein source in animal feed.[47]

It is essential for a processor to project the prices of the by-products it can produce to forecast accurately total project revenues. Even though this is difficult (because it requires an analysis of supply and demand conditions in another industry), these projections should take into account price levels and variability. If the realizable revenue and profit margin are small relative to the main product, then extensive price projections are not warranted. Nevertheless, estimates of a by-product's market are important because in some cases the economic importance of the by-product can become paramount. For example, several years ago a sugar manufacturer in a South American country developed a process for converting bagasse (sugarcane residue after extraction) into pulp for the production of paper. This process gave economic value to a previously unused by-product (before, it had a negative value because it cost the processor to dispose of the bagasse as waste). Changes in the international sugar market subsequently caused a drastic decline in sugar prices, while at the same time prices for paper products in the domestic market continued to increase. The shifts in the paper industry were so dramatic that the sugar refinery's profits from its bagasse sales exceeded its profits from processed sugar: in effect, bagasse became its primary product and sugar its by-product. The analyst must realize that, in keeping with agroindustry's intersectoral nature, the agroindustrial firm is in many businesses simultaneously and that a project's operating strategies must be adjusted according to the overall price dynamics.

Another aspect worth considering is the extent to which the variability in by-product price provides countercyclical or seasonal balancing to the variations in the primary products' prices. A further consideration is the possibility of the processor's using the by-products as energy sources. Because energy costs are rising, this use for by-products is of increasing economic importance. For example, a vegetable-oil processor visited by the author in a Central American country has used the cottonseed husks as boiler fuel (in sugar refining, bagasse can be similarly used). Some feedlots in the

47. E. Felton and Ray A. Goldberg, *The Broiler Industry of Guyana*, Report no. 4-373-015 (Boston: Harvard University, Graduate School of Business Administration, 1972).

United States recycle and convert their animal wastes into fuel, thereby simultaneously solving problems of waste disposal and environmental pollution. Similar, small-scale biogas plants are operating at the village level in India.

Salient points for project analysis

The following questions can be used by the analyst to assess a project's by-products.

What is the contribution to revenue of the by-products?
- Outputs?
- Unsold by-products with economic or nutritional value?
- Levels and variations in price of by-products?
- Any countercyclical or seasonal balancing to product's price variation from by-product sales?

Can by-products be used as energy sources for the processing operations?
- Additional investment required to convert by-product to energy source?
- How can such energy be used for the agroindustry's fuel needs?
- Can energy from by-product be sold outside the agroindustry?

Summary

Analysis of a project's processing operations derives from analyses of its procurement and marketing. Processing, however, links the project stages together and is the focal point of the investment; as such, it consists of additional elements.

A primary element in processing is technology; it must be tailored to fit the market's requirements. The nature of the production process will impose certain limits on choice of technology—for example, a minimum economic size. This may be a constraint for ssi's. Another critical selection criterion is cost, and here the analyst should examine the possibilities of the substitution of labor for capital as well as the relations between energy and raw material usage. Other criteria for technology selection include capacity use (the technology's contribution to minimizing the plant's down time because of seasonality) and management capabilities (to meet the supervisory and technical demands of the technology). The processor should also consider the potential nutritional consequences of the technology.

Another decision the processor must make is plant location. The value of locating near the markets or the producers of raw materials depends on the nature of the raw materials, the transformative process of the agroindustry, and the cost and reliability of the needed transport services. Labor supply, the availability of infrastructure, land costs, and the developmental effects of the project are additional considerations for plant location.

Inventory management also requires special attention because of the constraints of seasonality. The processor must determine the correct mix of raw and semiprocessed material and finished goods for optimal processing capacity. Adequate physical facilities are essential to prevent losses in product quantity and quality from pest and insect infestation or microbial growth. The raw material's seasonality accentuates the plant's needs for working capital and the inventory's exposure to price risks. The processor should explore the methods of handling both.

Processing supplies, particularly for packaging, are important in the manufacturing operation. The quantity and quality of the supply, the cost and dependability of delivery, and the nutritional effects of the packaging need to be assessed. Programming and control procedures should also be reviewed to ensure that production design and quality control will be adequately carried out. An implementation plan, project engineering, and a master production schedule should be drawn up before starting production. Finally, almost all agroindustries generate by-products. Because these can be important to the project's economics, the processor should estimate their financial contribution.

Appendix A

Illustrative Costs of Alternative Food-processing Technology

THE PURPOSE OF THIS APPENDIX is to provide the reader with additional information on the costs and operating characteristics of three common food-processing technologies: drying, freezing, and canning. The listed prices of equipment and costs of labor and energy should, of course, be updated and made site specific by any analyst wishing to cost a particular project. The data do, however, provide an idea of the relative orders of magnitude of the costs of different technological options and a methodology for making such calculations.

The appendix contains three main tables: A-1, which presents a comparison of different types of dryers (sun, cabinet, tunnel, continuous conveyor, belt trough, freeze, pneumatic conveyor, spray, drum, bin, and kiln); A-2, which compares various freezing methods (air blast, fluidized bed, liquid immersion, spray, and plate); and A-3, which includes different methods of canning (still retort, hydrostatic cooker, hydrolock system, direct flame sterilizer, aseptic sterilizer, sterilmatic retort, and orbitant).[1]

Before presenting these comparative tables, I will illustrate the methodology by which costs for the various technologies were developed; the estimated costs and performance data for cabinet dryers will serve as an example. Estimates are based on 1970 cost data given by Porter[2] and are updated by using the 1977 "M & S Equipment Cost Index."[3] According to these data, the following tabulation is obtained (all costs are in U.S. dollars):

1. The author expresses appreciation to Dr. Sam Yong, who carried out the literature review for the development of this appendix.
2. H. F. Porter, "Gas-Solid Systems," in *Chemical Engineers' Handbook*, 5th ed. (New York: McGraw-Hill, 1973), pp. 20–1 to 20–121.
3. In *Chemical Engineering*, vol. 84, no. 19 (September 12, 1977), p. 7.

Dryer volume (cubic feet)	Capacity (pounds of raw material daily)	1977 installed cost	1977 operating cost	
			Daily	Per pound of raw material
100	1,500	13,490	65.30	0.044
400	6,000	23,510	161.00	0.027
800	12,000	45,000	290.00	0.024

Capacity estimates are derived by the following assumptions:

- Fifty 5-square-foot trays per 100 cubic feet, or 750 pounds per 100 feet
- Loading of 3 pounds of raw material per square foot, or 15 pounds per tray
- Raw material contains 75 percent moisture (generally speaking, meat products contain 55–81 percent moisture, vegetables contain 75–90 percent moisture, and fruits contain 80–95 percent moisture), and most of this moisture is removed during drying at an overall drying rate of 0.2 pounds of water evaporated per square foot hourly, or 1 pound per tray hourly
- Seven hundred and fifty pounds of raw material at 75 percent moisture contain 560 pounds of water and, at 1 pound per tray hourly, a 100-cubic-foot dryer holding fifty trays will take 11 hours for drying and 0.5 hour for loading and unloading
- Two 12-hour cycles daily
- "Raw material" refers to prepared material ready for drying.

Porter[4] found that f.o.b. (free-on-board) costs of cabinet dryers in 1970 were $12 per cubic foot (dryers larger than 300 cubic feet) to $40 per cubic foot (dryers with 100 cubic feet). Costs included aluminized steel housing with 4 inches of insulation, circulating fan, and an air heater. Control instruments added $200–800, trays cost $2–4 per square foot, and trucks or racks cost $200–400. Installed cost is 50–100 percent over f.o.b. cost. According to these data, the following tabulation can be made (1970 installed cost is calculated at 50 percent over f.o.b.):

4. Porter, "Gas-Solid Systems," pp. 20–1 to 20–121.

Dryer volume (cubic feet)	1970 f.o.b. dryer cost	1970 f.o.b. cost of trays, trucks, controls	1970 installed cost
100	4,000	750 for trays (250 square feet at $3 a square foot) 300 for 1 truck/rack 400 for controls	8,175
400	4,800	3,000 for trays (1,000 square feet at $3 a square foot) 900 for 3 trucks 800 for controls	14,200
800	9,600	6,000 for trays (2,000 square feet at $3 a square foot) 1,800 for 6 trucks 800 for controls	27,300

The operating cost estimates (given in the first tabulation, above) are derived according to the following assumptions:

- Two man-hours to load/unload fifty trays or one truck in each 12-hour drying cycle
- Two and three-quarters pounds of steam or its equivalent in energy is required to evaporate 1 pound of water
- Maintenance cost of 3–5 percent of installed cost yearly for a 300-day year
- One-third man-hour to supervise the machine during drying
- Unskilled labor at an hourly wage of $4
- Three shifts and 24-hour operation
- No amortization has been taken into consideration.

By these assumptions, daily 1977 operating costs can be disaggregated in the following tabulation:

Dryer volume (cubic feet)	Trays (number)	Labor	Maintenance
100	50	48	1.80
400	200	96	3.13
800	400	160	6.00

The component 1977 daily energy costs are tabulated as follows:

Dryer volume (cubic feet)	*Energy*
100	15.50 (= 1,125 pounds of water evaporated × 2.75 pounds of steam × $5 per 1,000 pounds of steam)
400	61.90 (= 4,500 pounds of water evaporated × 2.75 pounds of steam × $5 per 1,000 pounds of steam)
800	123.75 (= 9,000 pounds of water evaporated × 2.75 pounds of steam × $5 per 1,000 pounds of steam)

The cost estimates for the other technologies were derived in similar fashion, but the details of the calculations and the sources for some data used will not, for reasons of space, be listed in the three comparative, summary tables that follow.

Table A-1. *Comparison of Selected Dryers*
(costs in U.S. dollars)

Dryer	Mode and scale of operation	1977 capital cost[a]	1977 operating cost[b]	Comment
Sun	Batch operation for small- to large-scale production of dried fruits, fish, and other piece-form foods	Negligible (for racks, trays, and the like)	High labor requirement but free energy; no maintenance problems	Loss of products from adverse changes in weather during drying season can be substantial; not suited to areas with cool or humid climate (or both); more destructive to provitamin A carotenes, vitamin C, and (possibly) riboflavin than mechanical dehydration; adding sulfite to fruits and vegetables to prevent browning causes large losses of thiamin but is beneficial to provitamin A and vitamin C retention; long drying time contributes to nutrient losses; products (such as dried fruits) have special accepted organoleptic characteristics difficult to reproduce in mechanical drying
Cabinet	Batch operation for small-scale production (1–20 metric tons daily) of such foods as dried vegetables, fruits, meat products, egg whites;	$13,000 for ¾ ton, $24,000 for 3 tons, $45,000 for 6 tons daily	High labor requirement for loading/unloading; labor cost is 55–75 percent of total operating cost; relatively low maintenance cost (simple op-	Long drying time because of slow removal of water (0.2 pounds hourly per square foot) contributes to high losses of nutrients and lower organoleptic quality; long drying time and relatively low drying temperature some-

	Suitability/Operation	Cost and labor	Quality/Comments
	can process almost any form of food (solids, liquids, or slurries)	eration); $0.024–.044 per pound raw material (65 percent moisture), $0.032–.057 per pound water removed	times present sanitary problems; suited to small-scale batch production of different products or as back-up dryer for sun drying during adverse weather
Tunnel	Semicontinuous operation for large-scale (10–50 tons daily) production of dried vegetables, fruits, meats, other piece-form foods; can process various solid foods with minor changes in operations	$58,000 for 7½ tons, $113,000 for 15 tons daily. Relatively high labor requirements for loading/unloading trucks; labor cost is 50 percent of total operating cost; relatively low maintenance cost; $0.023–.024 per pound raw material (75 percent moisture), $0.031–.032 per pound water removed	Long drying time contributes to higher losses of nutrients and lower organoleptic quality than other more advanced drying methods; sanitary problems are sometimes encountered
Continuous conveyor	Continuous operation for medium- to large-scale production of dried piece-form foods; best for large volumes of one product; not suited to different products in one plant	$125,000 for 15 tons, $208,000 for 30 tons, $280,000 for 46 tons, $431,000 for 92 tons daily. Low labor costs but skilled personnel required for operation and maintenance; labor cost is 5–20 percent of total operating cost; more efficient cost than cabinet or tunnel dryers; $0.01–.013 per pound raw material at	Because of shorter drying times, products with higher nutrient retention and better organoleptic quality are produced than those from tunnel or cabinet drying; fewer sanitary problems than with tunnel or cabinet drying

(Table continues on the following page.)

Table A-1 (*continued*)

Dryer	Mode and scale of operation	1977 capital cost[a]	1977 operating cost[b]	Comment
Continuous conveyor (*continued*)			75 percent moisture, $0.013–.017 per pound water removed	
Belt-trough	Continuous operation for medium- to large-scale production of dried, piece-form products; best for large volumes of one product; piece sizes must be small and uniform for efficient drying	2–3 times conveyor-dryer cost based on conveyor surface, but comparable in output	Similar to conveyor dryer (above)	Similar to conveyor dryer (above); because of short drying time (3–4 times faster than conveyor dryer), high-quality products with good nutrient retention are produced
Freeze	Batch operation for small- to medium-scale production; best for small volumes of piece-form foods with high market value (such as spices); can process almost any form of food (solids, liquids, or slurries)	$18,000 for 320 pounds, $34,000 for 1,120 pounds, $87,000 for 2 tons daily[c]	Relatively labor-intensive because of batch loading/unloading (similar to cabinet dryers, above); $0.035–.175 per pound raw material (75 percent moisture), $0.047–0.233 per pound water removed	In general, freeze drying can produce dried products with the best organoleptic quality and highest retention of nutrients; freeze-dried products suffer negligible shrinkage compared with other dried products and enjoy high consumer acceptance

168

Pneumatic conveyor	Batch or continuous operation for large-scale drying of powder or granules with low moisture content; best for operations requiring conveyance and classification during drying	$120,000 for 90 tons, $136,000 for 120 tons, $164,000 for 200 tons, $220,000 for 480 tons daily[d]	Low labor costs but skilled personnel required for maintenance and operation; $0.004 per pound raw material, $0.0133 per pound water removed	This dryer is used for materials that can be carried by high-velocity air (such as flour, grains, powder); because drying time is short, loss of nutrients is negligible and little adverse organoleptic change takes place
Rotary	Batch or continuous operation for medium- to large-scale drying of solids that are relatively free-flowing and granular (such as grains)	$122,000 for 16 tons, $182,000 for 28 tons, $264,000 for 48 tons, $363,000 for 75 tons daily[d]	Low labor costs but skilled personnel required for maintenance and operation; $0.005–.007 per pound raw material, $0.0166–.0233 per pound water removed	Similar to, but requiring less floor space than, pneumatic conveyor
Spray	Continuous operation for medium- to large-scale drying of fluids, slurries, and pastes; best for drying one product in large volumes	$330,000 for 11 tons, $495,000 for 32 tons, $644,000 for 64 tons, $825,000 for 144 tons daily[e]	Low labor costs but skilled personnel required for maintenance and operation; $0.005–.019 per pound raw material, $0.007–.0253 per pound water removed	Spray drying can produce products comparable in organoleptic quality and nutrient retention with those produced by freeze drying; in United States and other developed countries, most dried milk solids and whole egg solids are produced by spray drying (milk and egg must be pasteurized before spray-drying to kill pathogenic microorganisms)

(Table continues on the following page.)

Table A-1 (continued)

Dryer	Mode and scale of operation	1977 capital cost[a]	1977 operating cost[b]	Comment
Drum[f]	Continuous operation for small- to medium-scale drying of fluids, slurries, and pastes; best for one product	$44,750 for 1½ tons, $70,000 for 5 tons, $100,000 for 8 tons, $228,000 for 32 tons daily[e]	Same as for spray drying (above); $0.012–.04 per pound raw material, $0.016–.053 per pound water removed	In general, drum dryers produce products that are inferior in organoleptic and nutritive quality to spray-dried because of scorching and other problems; drum-dried milk, however, is often preferred over spray-dried milk for candy making (because of higher free fat content and heat-induced stabilization against oxidation) and for sausage making (because of higher water absorption); because of the flaky characteristics it gives, drum drying is still extensively used to make potato flakes and similar products; drum drying usually involves much smaller capital investment than spray drying—this may be advantageous when the drying operation is small, seasonal, or dependent on raw materials whose availability is not secure
Bin	Batch operation for finish drying (that is, to reduce moisture from 10 to 3 percent)	½–⅓ that of a cabinet dryer of similar size	½–⅓ that of a cabinet dryer, based on cost per pound water removed	During finish drying in bins, moisture is redistributed among the almost dry products, and, at the same time, most moisture is removed; this lowering and

of previously dried products; best for piece-form foods containing low moisture (such as grains, dried potato flakes)		redistribution is very important to the storage stability of dried foods
Kiln — Batch operation for small- to medium-scale drying of apple rings, hops, green fodder, and the like; used to dry food solids in areas where sun drying is impractical because of high humidity or cold climate or both	Same as for bin dryers (above) — Same as for bin dryers (above)	Because of the long drying time required, the nutritional and organoleptic quality of the products is probably inferior to that obtained by cabinet drying and comparable to that obtained by sun drying; sanitary problems occur

a. Dollar figures have been rounded to the nearest thousand.
b. Operating costs are obtained from previous tabulations (see text) and have been rounded to the nearest thousandth of a dollar (mill, or tenth of a cent); operating costs listed do not include amortization.
c. Cost of freezing equipment not included.
d. Raw material is assumed to contain only 30 percent moisture.
e. Liquid raw material contains 75 percent moisture.
f. Estimates are based on 1962 cost data given by Brown and others ["Drying Methods and Driers," in *Food Dehydration*, vol. 2, ed. W. B. Van Aredel and M. J. Copley (Westport, Conn.: Avi Publishing Co., 1964), p. 29] and are updated by using the 1977 "M & S Equipment Cost Index" [*Chemical Engineering*, vol. 84, no. 19 (September 12, 1977), p. 7].

Table A-2. *Comparison of Selected Freezers*
(costs in U.S. dollars)

Freezer	Mode and scale of operation	1977 capital cost[a]	1977 operating cost	Comment
Conventional air-blast	Batch operation for small- to large-scale production of frozen boxed foods (such as vegetables), poultry, fish; versatile in the variety of products it can process	$186,000 for 60 tons daily	High labor requirement for loading/unloading; low maintenance cost; $0.0183 per pound raw material	Capable of freezing almost anything that can be fit into them; because of slow freezing time,[b] high labor costs, low organoleptic quality of products, and high drip losses during thawing (which can cause nutrient losses), these freezers are being replaced by more advanced technology; they can, however, be economically used to freeze foods containing high solids (meats, for example) that are not highly sensitive to freezing damages and that have relatively low market value
Air-blast tunnel and conveyor tunnel	Batch or continuous operation for medium- to large-scale production of frozen whole poultry, fish, fish fillets, and the like (can freeze anything that can be adequately fit on conveyor or tray); best for continuous operation	$372,000 for 60 tons daily	High labor requirement for batch operation; labor requirement lower for continuous operation but still high compared to fluidized-bed freezing (below); $0.0122 per pound raw material	Faster than conventional air-blast freezers (see text) but still slower than other methods; most frequently used for high-solid foods not highly sensitive to freezing damages that cannot be adequately or economically frozen by more advanced methods (for example, whole poultry, boned fish fillets, whole fish); relatively long freezing time makes evaporation losses from unpackaged foods significant (alleviated by wrapping foods in thin plastic)

Method	Operation and scale	Capital cost	Labor/operating cost	Best suited to
Fluidized bed	Continuous operation for medium- to large-scale production of peas, shrimp, cut vegetables, and other small, individually frozen foods; method can process only foods that can be fluidized by air	$372,000 for 60 tons daily	Low labor requirement but skilled personnel required for operation and maintenance; $0.0079 per pound raw material	Best suited to continuous production of one product in large volumes (technical complexities occur in readjusting machine for different products); to achieve efficient freezing, raw material must consist of uniform (machine cut) pieces that are not easily ripped apart by high-velocity air; fast freezing makes product quality comparable to that from liquid-immersion freezing and spray freezing; individually frozen pieces have high consumer utility
Liquid-immersion (brine)	Batch or continuous operation for small- to large-scale production of frozen canned foods or whole fish	Data unavailable (but much cheaper than freon immersion freezer)	Relatively high labor requirement for batch operation; cost probably similar to that of conventional air-blast freezer	Best suited to freezing foods not adversely affected by brine (for example, canned fruit juice or whole fish); fast freezing rate because of good contact between brine and food material and because brine is a better medium for heat transfer than air; used extensively to freeze canned, concentrated fruit juices and whole fish (in factory boats)
Liquid-immersion (freon)	Continuous operation for small- to large-scale production of individually frozen foods such as shrimp,	$532,000 for 60 tons daily	Very high operating cost because of loss of expensive freezant; $0.0265 per pound raw material	Best suited to individual freezing of delicate foods that have high market value and cannot be adequately frozen by other methods; extremely rapid freezing rates yield frozen products (Table continues on the following page.)

Table A-2 (continued)

Freezer	Mode and scale of operation	1977 capital cost[a]	1977 operating cost	Comment
Liquid-immersion (freon) (continued)	scallops, onion rings			with high organoleptic quality; individually frozen pieces have high consumer utility; large-scale operation is required to offset high capital cost
Spray	Continuous operation for small- to large-scale production of individually frozen foods such as fish, poultry, meat patties; versatile—adaptable to various production rates and product sizes; small space requirement	$106,000 for 60 tons daily (if liquid nitrogen or carbon dioxide is used); $532,000 for 60 tons daily (if liquid or solid carbon dioxide is used with recovery system)	Very high operating costs in system without freezant recovery (liquid nitrogen or carbon dioxide is very expensive); $0.0506 per pound raw material (if liquid nitrogen is used); $0.038 per pound (if carbon dioxide is used); $0.0152 per pound (if carbon dioxide is used with recovery system)	Relatively low capital cost without freezant recovery system makes these freezers best suited to small- to medium-scale, seasonal production of high-quality products (probably products with best quality among all freezing methods) with high market value; because of the high capital cost of the recovery system, spray freezers with freezant recovery systems are economically feasible only if large-scale production can be assured throughout the year; individually frozen pieces have high consumer utility

| Plate | Batch operation for small- to medium-scale production of packaged frozen foods such as fish fillets, meats, fruits | $372,000 for 60 tons daily | High labor costs for loading and unloading of food materials; $0.0107 per pound of raw material | Good contact between cold plates and packaged food materials gives this method the fastest freezing rate for packages filled with food materials; because of the pressure applied on the plates, uniform, well-shaped products with minimum voids can be manufactured; not suited to freezing packages with much dead air space; used extensively to produce "fish sticks" (bits and pieces, as well as fillets, of fish are frozen into large slabs with application of pressure in plate freezer; the frozen slab is sawed into desired sizes and batter is applied; the ready-to-fry product is frozen again) |

a. Cost estimates are based on 1976 data provided by J. R. Behnke ["Freezing: End-Product Quality Is as Important an Investment as Operating Costs in Selecting a Freezing System," *Food Technology*, vol. 30, no. 12 (1976), p. 32] and 1971 data from A. W. Ruff ["Freezing Systems: Investment and Operating Costs," *Food Engineering*, vol. 43, no. 9 (September 1971), p. 76]; as before, data have been updated by using the 1977 "M & S Equipment Cost Index."

b. A comparison of freezing times for small fruits and vegetables by different freezing methods and the product form they require, based on data provided by C. L. Rasmussen and R. L. Olson ["Freezing Methods as Related to Costs and Quality," *Food Technology*, vol. 26, no. 12 (1972), p. 32], is as follows: conventional air-blast (10-ounce packages), 3–5 hours; plate (10-ounce packages), ½–1 hour; air-blast conveyor tunnel (individual pieces in bulk), 20–30 minutes; fluidized bed or tray (individual pieces in bulk), 5–10 minutes; cryogenic (individual pieces in bulk), ½–1 minute.

Table A-3. *Comparison of Selected Types of Canning Equipment*
(costs in U.S. dollars)

Canning method	Mode and scale of operation	1977 Capital cost[a]	1977 operating cost	Comment
Still retort	Batch operation for small- to medium-scale production of canned or bottled foods; versatile in the variety of products able to process	$14,000 for 8–16 tons daily; $16,000 for 12–24 tons daily	High labor requirement for loading and unloading; low maintenance cost; $0.0029–.0077 per pound raw material	Can process a variety of can sizes and products; the sterilization time, however, is long and the canned products have poor organoleptic quality and low nutrient retention compared with products of more advanced methods; oldest and probably most commonly used equipment for commercial sterilization; use of laminated, flexible pouches instead of cans or bottles can significantly reduce sterilization time and improve product quality
Hydrostatic cooker	Continuous operation for large scale production of canned or bottled foods; most suited to processing one particular food product in large volume	$633,000 for 100–200 tons daily	Skilled labor required for operation and maintenance; low manual labor requirement; 0.0019–.003 per pound raw material	Suited to handling containers susceptible to thermal shock (such as glass bottles); shorter sterilization time than still retorts (particularly for nonviscous food materials) because of agitating motion of the conveyor during sterilization; accordingly, yields products with better organoleptic and nutritive quality than those from still retorts; rather complicated engineering

176

Hydrolock system	Similar to hydrostatic cookers	Not available (probably similar to that for hydrostatic cookers)	Not available (similar to that for hydrostatic cookers)	Similar in performance to hydrostatic cookers; also suited to processing laminated flexible pouches
Direct-flame sterilizers	Continuous operation for large-scale production of canned vegetables (particularly mushrooms); can process only small cans	Not available	Not available (similar to that for hydrostatic cookers)	These sterilizers are suited to processing nonviscous foods in small containers; because of short sterilization time (shorter than hydrolock or hydrostatic systems), products with very good organoleptic quality and nutrient retention can be made; because of build-up of internal pressure during heating, only small cans can be processed satisfactorily
Aseptic sterilizer	Continuous operation for large-scale production of canned or bottled (or laminated pouch-packaged) fluid foods	$1,–30,000 for 200 tons daily	Low manual labor requirement but skilled labor required for operation and maintenance; high maintenance cost; $0.0018 per pound raw material	Extremely short sterilization time; yields best organoleptic quality and nutrient retention among all canning methods, but can process only fluid foods
Sterilmatic retort and orbitant	Continuous operation for medium- to large-scale production of canned foods	Not available	Not available (similar to that for hydrostatic cookers)	Similar to hydrostatic cookers

a. Cost estimates are based on data provided by A. K. Robins and Co. for still retorts; by F. K. Lawler ["The French Build Efficient Canneries," *Food Engineering*, vol. 32, no. 3 (March 1960), p. 64] for hydrostatic cookers; and by the editors of *Food Engineering* ["Aseptic Milk Makes N. American Debut," vol. 47, no. 9 (September 1975), p. 15] for aseptic sterilizing equipment. As in the other comparative tables, figures are updated by using the 1977 "M & S Equipment Cost Index."

Appendix B

Checklist of Critical Questions for Agroindustrial Project Analysis

IN THIS APPENDIX the "salient points for project analysis" listed at the end of the sections of chapters 2–4 are compiled in fuller form and greater detail. It is hoped that this inventory of pertinent, analytical questions will not only serve to review the issues discussed in this book but will also furnish the practicing analyst with a useful tool for the assessment of agroindustrial projects in the field.

The organization of the questions herein parallels the organization of the book in its chapter and section headings.

THE MARKETING FACTOR

Consumer Analysis

Who are the potential consumers?
- ☐ What are their economic characteristics? income levels? variability?
- ☐ What are their sociocultural characteristics? ethnicity? language? class? education?
- ☐ What are their demographic characteristics? regional location? urban or rural? age? sex?
- ☐ What are the market segments?
- ☐ What are the product's options among these segments?
- ☐ What do the segments imply for the marketing plan?

Why would consumers buy the product?
- ☐ What physiological, sociological, or psychological needs would the product meet?
- ☐ What are the expressed reasons for purchasing? sensory appeal? sustenance? status? convenience? necessity?

☐ What is the relative importance of the needs and reasons?

☐ What are the implications of these for the distribution options and the marketing plan?

How would consumers buy the product?

☐ Which individuals would make the purchase decision and what are their roles in the decisionmaking unit (DMU)?

☐ What method of disseminating information to each member of the DMU would be appropriate?

☐ Would the purchases be on impulse or planned?

☐ Would the purchases be made frequently or seldom?

☐ Would the purchases be seasonal?

☐ Where would the purchases be made?

☐ What are the implications of the buying process for the marketing plan?

What market information and methods of data collection are needed?

☐ What are the data needs?

☐ What are the data sources? primary? secondary?

☐ What were the methods of data collection? formal? informal?

☐ How valid was the research design for data collection?

☐ How reliable are the data sources and collection methods?

☐ What is the cost of collecting additional data?

☐ Do the benefits expected from the incremental information outweigh the additional costs of data collection?

☐ Will small-scale industries (SSI's) need assistance to conduct market research?

Analysis of the Competitive Environment

What is the product's market structure?

☐ Who are the competitors? public or private? regional, national, or international? old or new?

☐ What are the effects of substitute products?

☐ What is the chance of raw material suppliers' integrating forward, or of distributors' integrating backward?

☐ How many competing firms are there?

☐ Where are the competitors located relative to markets and raw materials?

☐ What size are the competitors' assets and sales?
☐ What is each firm's market share?
☐ How have these shares changed over recent years?

What is the basis of competition in the industry?
☐ How sensitive are these consumers to price?
☐ How prevalent is price discounting?
☐ How sensitive are consumers to product quality?
☐ How do consumers define quality?
☐ How sensitive are consumers to brand names?
☐ What kind of special services are given to distributors or retailers, and how often?
☐ At what stage of the product life cycle (PLC) is the industry?
☐ How significant are the barriers to entry from economies of scale? absolute cost advantages? vertical system control? brand franchise?

How do institutional constraints affect the competitive environment?
☐ What are the effects of economic constraints or incentives? tariffs? quotas? export promotion bonuses? tax credits?
☐ What are the effects of health constraints? sanitary standards?
☐ What are the effects of political constraints? price controls? subsidies? direct government intervention? industrial licensing?
☐ What are the effects of legal constraints? antitrust legislation? patent requirements?

The Marketing Plan

Was the product adequately designed?
☐ What product characteristics do consumers want?
☐ Which characteristics are most important?
☐ Does the cost of improvements in quality keep the product within the consumer's price range?
☐ Have the product's concept and prototype been tested with consumers?
☐ Do SSI's need government assistance with product design?
☐ What were the results of the product's design tests?
☐ Were further adjustments to the design made?

□ Was the final product market tested?
□ What were the results?
□ Does the end product meet consumer needs?

Was the appropriate pricing strategy adopted?
□ Is cost-plus pricing feasible?
□ Are prices regulated?
□ How is the markup calculated?
□ Is penetration pricing needed to overcome entry barriers?
□ Would low prices expand the market adequately to offset the lower profit margins?
□ Would predatory or preemptive pricing be legally or socially responsible?
□ Would loss-leader pricing expand the sales volume of other company products enough to offset the sacrifice on the loss leader?
□ Is the product sufficiently new, differentiated, and lacking in competition to permit a skimming price strategy?
□ Is there an industry price leader?
□ If so, what are the benefits of following or deviating from the leader's pattern?
□ Are prices administered legally or through cartels?
□ Are prices subsidized?
□ Are prices determined by supply and demand?
□ What are the pricing reference points?
□ Can long-term contracts or futures markets be used to reduce the uncertainty of price variability?
□ Will the pricing strategy work, given the competitors' strategy?
□ How does the firm expect the pricing strategy to change over time?

Was the right promotional strategy formulated?
□ What is the market-segment audience?
□ What differences are there among members of the DMU?
□ Will promotion be directed toward end consumers as a "pull" strategy?
□ Will promotion be directed toward distributors as a "push" strategy?
□ Is the promotional message consistent with analyses of the consumers and the competitive environment?

☐ What are the consumers' informational needs?

☐ What information is being supplied by competitors?

☐ What does the firm expect the promotional message to do?

☐ Will the consumer misinterpret the message or misuse the product?

☐ How will increased consumption affect the nutritional well-being of low-income consumers?

☐ Will the promotion stimulate primary or secondary demand?

☐ Would branding increase selective demand?

☐ Are quality-control procedures at the processing and procurement stages adequate to permit branding?

☐ Is the promotional vehicle an indirect communication or direct, personal selling?

☐ Are the promotional vehicles consistent with the characteristics of the selected audience?

☐ What portion of the audience will be reached by the vehicle and how frequently?

☐ What is the cost potential of promotional vehicles relative to their coverage?

☐ Would the cost-benefit of the promotion improve if a combination of vehicles were used?

Will the distribution system adequately link the manufacturer to the marketplace?

☐ What is the structure of the distribution system? length of the channels?

☐ How many distributors are at each level of the channels?

☐ What kinds of distributors are at the wholesale and retail levels?

☐ Who is performing the logistical functions (transport, assembly, repackaging, storage, inventory management)?

☐ Who is performing the service functions (financing, promotion, information collection)?

☐ Should the firm use the existing institutions for distribution or perform some functions directly through forward vertical integration?

☐ Can ssi's realize economies by performing these functions collectively?

☐ What are the cost, quality, and dependability of existing distribution services?

☐ Are the distributors capable and willing to meet the consumers' needs?
☐ Where is the power in the distribution channels?
☐ Why is the power there?
☐ How will the power distribution affect the project?
☐ What capital and managerial resources would the firm require for forward integration?
☐ What are the social, political, or legal barriers to integration?
☐ Has the distribution system adopted intensive, selective, or exclusive retail outlets?
☐ Is that choice consistent with the characteristics of the product, the market segment, and the consumers' buying processes?

Are the elements of the marketing mix integrated into a viable marketing plan?
☐ Are the marketing elements internally consistent?
☐ How will the marketing plan for this product affect other products in the company's line?
☐ Is the marketing plan compatible with the company's financial, organizational, production, and procurement plans?
☐ What does the firm expect the competitive response to the marketing plan will be?
☐ How will the marketing effort respond to the competitive response?

Demand Forecasting

Are the data on which the forecasts are based sound?
☐ Are the data prices consistent?
☐ Are the units of measure standardized?
☐ Are the data disaggregated sufficiently to project market-segment demand and total demand?
☐ Have all the relevant secondary data sources been used?
☐ Was market research used to generate primary data?
☐ How were the data collected?
☐ Are the data representative?
☐ Have the data been verified?
☐ What are the underlying assumptions of the data projections?

☐ How sensitive are sales and profit estimates to changes in the assumptions?

Are the forecasting methods appropriate?
☐ Who provided the judgmental estimates?
☐ What was the basis of their expertise?
☐ Can other relevant opinions be gathered?
☐ If trend projections were made, how representative were the historical series?
☐ Were seasonal, secular, cyclical, or random variations in the series considered?
☐ Were moving averages or exponential weighting techniques employed?
☐ If a regression analysis was used, was it simple or multiple, arithmetic or logarithmic?
☐ Were estimates made of price and income elasticity of demand?
☐ If an econometric model was used, what were the variables?
☐ What causal relationships are assumed in the model?
☐ Are these assumptions reasonable?
☐ Is the accuracy of the projection acceptable, given the risk and uncertainty?
☐ How much could the accuracy be increased by using a more sophisticated technique?
☐ Would the incremental accuracy justify the added cost?
☐ Is the previously used forecasting method still appropriate?
☐ How do the possible forecasting techniques rank in cost, accuracy, skill requirements, data requirements, and speed?

The Procurement Factor

Adequate Quantity

What was the total production pattern?
☐ What were the production levels? by region? for the past five years?
☐ How variable was output?
☐ What factors affected the variability?

What is the usage pattern of the area planted?
☐ How much variation has there been in planted area?
☐ How much land is economically arable but uncultivated?

☐ What trends are there toward opening up new land for planting?

☐ How productive is the new land relative to the old?

☐ To what extent have farmers shifted among crops?

☐ How much shifting is agronomically feasible?

☐ What are the nutritional consequences of crop shifts?

☐ How much land or labor has urbanization or industrialization absorbed?

☐ What effect will land-reform programs have on the area planted?

What is the crop yield?

☐ How variable have yields been? why have they varied?

☐ To what extent do farmers use agrochemicals?

☐ To what extent do they use improved seed varieties?

☐ What barriers (for example, credit, price, distribution) exist to the increased usage of these inputs?

☐ How can these barriers to usage be overcome?

☐ Do the farmers know how to use these inputs?

☐ Do they receive technical assistance? how much? of what kind? from whom?

How profitable is the crop?

☐ How profitable is the crop for the farmer?

☐ How does that differ from returns on other crops?

☐ What does it cost the farmer to produce the crop?

☐ How does that differ from costs of other crops?

☐ How risky is the crop for the farmer?

How sensitive is supply to production changes?

☐ How would a change of 10 percent (or more) in area planted affect total supply?

☐ What price incentive is required to increase acreage?

☐ How would a change of 10 percent (or more) in yields affect total supply?

☐ What would it cost to increase the yield?

☐ What is the probability of increases in area or yield?

Is the raw material a by-product of another agroindustry?

☐ What is the supply of the primary product from which the by-product is derived?

☐ What is the market demand for the primary product?
☐ Are external supplies of the primary or by-product available through imports if domestic shortfalls occur?
☐ Are there alternative forms of the raw material?

What is the on-farm consumption?
☐ What percentage of the crop is consumed on the farm?
☐ How would increased output or higher prices affect the amount flowing into the commercial channels?
☐ How would increased off-farm sales affect the nutritional well-being of the farm families? of landless laborers?

How is the product consumed?
☐ Is the raw material consumed fresh or processed?
☐ What are the proportions and trends for usage?
☐ How complementary are the product's uses in fresh and processed forms?

What is the animal versus human usage?
☐ Is the raw material consumed by animals and humans?
☐ What are the proportions and trends for usage?
☐ What are the government's priorities for usage?

What are the industrialization options for the raw material?
☐ How many end products are produced from the raw material?
☐ What is the demand for these various uses?
☐ What are the price differentials for the raw material among these different uses?

Is there competition in procurement among similar agroindustries?
☐ How many firms procure the same product?
☐ How much raw material do they purchase?
☐ How does their buying power compare with that of the project?

What are the probable crop losses?
☐ How much of the harvested crop is lost because of rodent or insect damage, poor handling, or inadequate storage?
☐ What measures could reduce these losses?
☐ Do proposed production schemes have adequate on- and off-farm storage facilities?

Acceptable Quality

What are the market's qualitative requirements?
- ☐ What market segments will be served?
- ☐ How quality conscious are they?
- ☐ What characteristics do they use to define quality?
- ☐ What do they pay for different levels of quality?

What is the quality of the farm supply?
- ☐ What seed varieties are used?
- ☐ Will the resultant characteristics of the raw material be consistent with the processed product's qualitative needs?
- ☐ What other quality-oriented inputs are used?
- ☐ Do farmers have adequate knowledge of these inputs to achieve the desired levels of quality?
- ☐ Will technical assistance be needed? of what kind? from whom?

How does handling and transport affect quality?
- ☐ Have harvesting and transport personnel been trained in handling techniques that will minimize damage to produce?
- ☐ Will transport methods and delays damage the produce?
- ☐ What nutrient losses and adverse changes in appearance will occur?

How does storage affect quality?
- ☐ What are the storage facilities and fumigation practices?
- ☐ Will they prevent damage to produce (including nutrient loss)?

What inputs or services can increase quality control?
- ☐ Should the processing plant provide seeds, agrochemicals, storage, drying, or other services?
- ☐ What would be the cost?
- ☐ How much would quality improve?
- ☐ What would be the economic benefits of these measures?

What qualitative specifications and inspection procedures should be instituted?
- ☐ Are qualitative standards for the raw material specified?
- ☐ Are there means to communicate the specifications for the raw material to the farmers?

☐ Are there procedures for crop inspection?
☐ Are there adequately trained inspection personnel?

What quality control would result from backward integration?
☐ How much additional quality control would be gained if the processor integrated backward to assume the production, storage, transport, and handling functions?
☐ How do these benefits compare with the cost and with the alternatives for quality control?

Appropriate Timing

What is the seasonal harvesting pattern?
☐ When is the crop harvested (or the animal slaughtered)?
☐ Would different seed varieties (or livestock breeds) lengthen or spread the flow of raw material to the plant?
☐ Would staggered planting (or altered feeding patterns) lengthen or spread the flow of raw material to the plant?
☐ What would it cost to adjust the flow period?
☐ How do the costs compare with the benefits of a more even flow?

What facilities are required by the seasonal pattern?
☐ What drying (or corral) capacity will be needed to absorb the harvest (or animals)?
☐ What will be the peak of the raw material inventory?
☐ How much storage capacity will be needed for peak inventory?
☐ Can the firm rent space for peak inventory, thereby reducing the overall investment?

How perishable is the raw material?
☐ When must the crop be harvested (or animal be slaughtered) to avoid deterioration of quality?
☐ How soon after harvest must the crop be processed to avoid esthetic or nutritional damage?

What facilities are necessitated by the raw material's perishability?
☐ Are there adequate harvesting, transport, and storage services?
☐ Can these services meet the constraints of the material's period of perishability?

☐ Can special treatments (for example, freezing, precooling, waxing) reduce perishability?

When and for how long will the raw material be available?
☐ Is the crop (or breed) new to the area?
☐ How long a period is needed to ensure agronomic suitability (or acclimatization)?
☐ How long is the planting-to-harvest period (or breeding cycle)?
☐ How will farmers be financed during this period?
☐ Do cultural practices threaten the viability of the crop (or livestock)?
☐ What is the yield pattern over the life span of the crop (for perennial crops and breeding animals)?
☐ How will this pattern affect flow of the raw material?
☐ What is the risk of suppliers' switching among crops or land uses?
☐ Are there multiple sources of the raw material?

Reasonable Cost

How do supply and demand affect the cost of raw material?
☐ How strong is the demand from competing users of the raw material?
☐ How will the project affect raw material demand and prices?
☐ What are the supply projections under varying prices?

What are the farmers' opportunity costs?
☐ What are the land's alternative uses?
☐ How profitable are these activities?

How do structural factors affect costs?
☐ What margins do the middlemen between farmer and factory receive?
☐ Would it be cost effective and organizationally and politically feasible for the factory to perform these intermediary functions?

How do logistical services affect raw material costs?
☐ What are the farmers' transport charges?
☐ What portion of the price on delivery is the transport charge?

How does governmental involvement affect raw material costs?
- ☐ Is there a support price?
- ☐ Are services or inputs subsidized?

Should spot prices be used?
- ☐ What are the prevailing spot prices?
- ☐ How have they varied annually and across years?
- ☐ Do competitors use spot prices?

Are multiple sources a potential pricing mechanism?
- ☐ Can the plant use multiple crops for the raw material?
- ☐ How comparable are crops' price levels and variability?
- ☐ What is the lowest cost combination?
- ☐ What organizational or technical problems for processing are caused by multiple sources?

How do support prices affect pricing?
- ☐ Is there a governmental minimum support price for the crop?
- ☐ What percentage of the crop flow is affected by this program?
- ☐ How comparable are the support price and the spot price?

Is contracting a desirable pricing mechanism?
- ☐ Are production contracts currently used by farmers?
- ☐ What should the contract terms be for quantity, quality, delivery, technical and financial assistance, and price terms?
- ☐ How long a period should the contract cover?
- ☐ Will the farmers comply with the contract terms?

Are joint ventures feasible and desirable?
- ☐ Are farmers interested in investing in the plant?
- ☐ Will this increase the certainty of supply or lower the raw material costs?
- ☐ What socioeconomic benefits would investment bring to the farmers?

Would backward integration lower costs of raw material?
- ☐ Could the plant integrate vertically backward and absorb transport or production or both?
- ☐ Would that lower the raw material costs?

What does the sensitivity analysis of raw material costs reveal?
- ☐ How would a 10 or 20 percent change in raw material costs affect profits and return on investment?
- ☐ What is the likelihood of such changes occurring?

Organization of the Procurement System

What are the number, size, and location of the operators in the structure of the existing system?
- ☐ How many producers, transporters, and buyers operate in the existing system?
- ☐ What are the implications of these numbers for the organization and control of a procurement system?
- ☐ What percentage of total marketed produce does each participant handle?
- ☐ How do their production techniques and needs differ?
- ☐ How differently must the plant interact with large and small suppliers?
- ☐ Where are the suppliers located?
- ☐ What implications will the geographical dispersion of producers have for plant location, logistical control, and the vulnerability of agronomic supply?

What is the suppliers' crop mix?
- ☐ What crops do the farmers grow?
- ☐ Do they specialize?
- ☐ To what extent do they shift among crops?

What are the patterns of land ownership?
- ☐ How much land is owned, rented, or sharecropped?
- ☐ How will differences in ownership affect farmers' relations with the processing plant?
- ☐ How mobile are the farmers?

What are the routes, timing, and accessibility of the raw material's flow?
- ☐ What are the raw material's flow channels?
- ☐ How much flows through these channels?

☐ When does it flow through?
☐ Can the flow meet the project's requirements?

What does the analysis of channel power reveal?
   ☐ How much power does each participant in the system have?
   ☐ How is it spread?
   ☐ What is the basis of power for each participant?
   ☐ What is the basis and strength of the project's power?

Should producers integrate vertically backward?
   ☐ How much will control of quantity, quality, and timing improve with integration?
   ☐ How far back should the producers integrate?
   ☐ How much additional fixed investment will be required to integrate?
   ☐ How much additional working capital?
   ☐ How might integration reduce the project's flexibility in obtaining sources of raw material?
   ☐ What are the economic and operational risks of a decrease in this flexibility?
   ☐ How will integration affect variable and fixed costs?
   ☐ How will integration affect the plant's break-even point?
   ☐ Is integration politically feasible or socially desirable?

Are there producers' organizations?
   ☐ How organized are producers?
   ☐ What are the goals and activities of existing producers' organizations?
   ☐ What are the barriers to organization?
   ☐ What incentives can the agroindustry provide to facilitate organization?
   ☐ How can the producers' organization be a vehicle for communication between factory and farmer?
   ☐ How can the producers' organization transmit services or quality-control functions?
   ☐ How can the producers' organization aid in economic bargaining?

Should farmers integrate vertically forward?
   ☐ What are the financial and managerial requirements for such integration?
   ☐ What are the benefits?

The Processing Factor

Selection of Processing Technology

Is the processing technology consistent with the qualitative requirements of the marketplace?
- ☐ Will the technology match the qualitative standards of the selected market segments?
- ☐ Will the incremental revenue from higher quality justify the increased investment in technology?
- ☐ Will the technology for the local market meet consumer requirements in the export market?

What constraints are imposed on technology selection by the technical requirements of the transformative process?
- ☐ How many forms of technology can meet the requirements of the process?
- ☐ Do these requirements dictate a minimum economic scale of operation?
- ☐ Are the sales forecasts consistent with this required minimum volume?

Which technology has the lowest socioeconomic costs?
- ☐ What are the relative costs of alternative mixes of capital and labor?
- ☐ Do the private and social costs of these factors differ?
- ☐ Are there component processes in the technological package that could operate more economically manually?
- ☐ Are there functions within the agroindustrial system that could be performed by ssi's?
- ☐ Can new technologies be developed that will be more appropriate to the country's factor endowment?
- ☐ Can costs of technology be minimized by buying secondhand equipment?
- ☐ What are the estimated energy requirements of alternative technologies relative to energy costs, supply, and sources?
- ☐ Can energy sources be derived from biomass?
- ☐ How significantly will the chosen technology economize on raw materials?

How will the technology affect use of project capacity?
- ☐ To what extent can the technology be adjusted to process other products and lengthen the project's operating period?
- ☐ What are the costs and benefits of such an adjustment?

How well does the technology fit with the firm's managerial capability?
- ☐ Will supervisory demands be excessive?
- ☐ Will technical demands be excessive?
- ☐ How can the technology be adjusted to reduce these demands?

What are the technology's nutritional consequences?
- ☐ How will processing affect the quality and quantity of the food product's proteins, carbohydrates, fats, vitamins, and minerals?
- ☐ How can the technology be adjusted to minimize nutrient loss?
- ☐ Can the technology improve the product's nutritional value through fortification, nutrient concentration, or by-product usage?

Plant Location

Do the raw material, market, and transport factors support the proposed location?
- ☐ How perishable and fragile is the firm's product?
- ☐ Will the processing increase or decrease the weight or volume of the raw material?
- ☐ How significant are transport costs and what are their foreseeable changes?
- ☐ If supplies or markets are scattered, how do the transport savings from multiple plants compare with the economies of scale from a single plant?
- ☐ How significant are transport costs relative to total product value?
- ☐ How adequate are the supply and quality of existing transport facilities?
- ☐ Should the plant develop its own transport services?

Is there an adequate labor supply at the location?
- ☐ Are the plant's requirements for unskilled labor compatible with the local supply?

☐ Can the plant recruit skilled technicians and professional managers at the proposed location?

☐ Will the plant need to offer special recruiting incentives?

Is the infrastructure at the location acceptable?

☐ How does the plant's incremental demand for electricity and steam compare with the projected supply?

☐ How many interruptions have there been to power supply in the past and how serious were they?

☐ What will the energy services cost?

☐ How does the plant's incremental demand for cooling, processing, and potable water compare with the actual and potential quantity and quality of the supply?

☐ What will the water cost?

☐ What are the effluent requirements and does the infrastructure adequately avoid pollution?

☐ Are there adequate fire-protection facilities?

☐ Is the transport infrastructure acceptable?

☐ Are the housing, educational, health, and recreational facilities adequate for plant personnel?

☐ How does the cost of remedying infrastructural deficiencies compare with site advantages?

What will the plant's land cost?

☐ How do the prices for a square meter of land compare among various sites?

☐ What is the rate of the land's appreciation?

☐ Can the firm purchase adequate land to allow for future expansion?

☐ Will future urbanization create transport congestion and increase costs?

What will be the developmental effects of the location?

☐ What direct and indirect employment will be generated?

☐ How will the project's location affect the income of low-income groups?

☐ What will be the developmental benefits for the region?

☐ Are fiscal or other governmental incentives available?

Inventory Management

What will be the best storage capacities for raw materials and finished goods?
- ☐ How quickly must the product be processed?
- ☐ How does the processing affect its storability?
- ☐ Can the product be semiprocessed to reduce the investment for the inventory of finished goods and extend the plant's use of its capacity?
- ☐ What are the comparative spatial and qualitative requirements for the inventory of the raw material and the finished goods?
- ☐ Is there adequate inventory capacity for processing supplies and equipment repair parts?

Are the physical facilities adequate?
- ☐ What are the potential quantitative and qualitative losses in the inventories of raw material and finished goods?
- ☐ What are the economic costs and benefits of adjusting facilities for inventory handling and storage to reduce these losses?
- ☐ Are the storage facilities effectively located relative to suppliers of raw material and distributors of finished goods?

Have the requirements for working capital and the inventory price risks been adequately analyzed?
- ☐ What are the working capital needs for seasonal procurement of the raw material?
- ☐ Is it possible to hedge against price risks on an existing futures market?
- ☐ What are the advantages and disadvantages of buying raw materials from a wholesaler throughout the year rather than stockpiling them at harvest time?
- ☐ Is it possible to achieve price protection for inventory through advance contracts?

Supplies for Processing

Where should the plant procure its ancillary supplies (packaging, ingredients, chemicals)?
- ☐ Can they be obtained locally in adequate quantity and quality when needed and at a reasonable cost?
- ☐ What will be the foreign exchange requirements, delivery delay risks, additional transport costs, and import duties of imported supplies?
- ☐ How can the processor help develop local suppliers' capabilities?
- ☐ What would be the economic, technical, and managerial feasibility of the plant's integrating to produce its own supplies?

What are the nutritional effects of the ancillary materials?
- ☐ What packaging is needed to preserve the product's nutritional quality?
- ☐ How will the packaging affect the product's price and consumption by lower-income groups?

Programming and Control

Is there a clear and systematic implementation plan?
- ☐ Are each of the postinvestment and preproduction steps delineated?
- ☐ Have programming techniques such as Gantt charts, Critical Path Method (CPM), or Project Evaluation and Review Technique (PERT) been used?

Has project engineering been carried out diagrammatically?
- ☐ Have general functional layouts been made?
- ☐ Have flow diagrams of materials been designed?
- ☐ Have production line diagrams been specified?
- ☐ Have transport, utility, communications, and manpower layouts been set forth?

Does a master schedule for procurement and processing exist?
- ☐ Has the seasonal availability of the raw material been considered?

☐ Has the possibility of the plant's working multiple shifts been explored?

☐ Have alternative uses of the production capacity been examined?

Are there systematic quality-control procedures for raw materials, work in process, and finished goods?

☐ Is there an inspection system for the raw material as it is being grown?

☐ Are contamination levels, packaging integrity, temperature, and chemical composition controlled?

☐ Are sampling procedures designated?

☐ Do laboratory testing facilities exist?

☐ Can nutritional quality be verified?

☐ Are corrective procedures specified?

By-products

What is the contribution to revenue of the by-products?

☐ What are the outputs?

☐ Are there unsold by-products that have an economic or nutritional value?

☐ What are the price levels and variations of the by-products?

☐ Do the by-product sales provide any countercyclical or seasonal balancing to variations in primary product prices?

Can the by-products be used as energy sources for the processing operations?

☐ What additional investment would be required to convert the by-product to an energy source?

☐ Can the energy be used to meet the agroindustry's own fuel needs?

☐ Can the energy from by-products be sold outside the agroindustry?

Bibliography

The following works augment the sources supporting the text of the book; they are arranged by chapter and, within these sections, by subject. The word "processed" describes works that are reproduced by mimeograph, xerography, or any means other than conventional typesetting and printing; such works may not be cataloged or commonly available through libraries, or may be subject to restricted circulation.

1. An Overview

Financial analysis

Blecke, Curtis. *Financial Analysis for Decision-making.* Englewood Cliffs, N.J.: Prentice-Hall, 1966.

Caiden, Naomi J., and Aaron Wildovsky. *Planning and Budgeting in Poor Countries.* New York: John Wiley and Sons, 1974.

Davenport, Robert W. *Financing the Small Manufacturer in Developing Countries.* New York: McGraw-Hill, 1967.

Dearden, John, and John Shank. *Financial Accounting and Reporting: A Contemporary Analysis.* Englewood Cliffs, N.J.: Prentice-Hall, 1975.

Goodman, Sam R. *Financial Analysis for Marketing Decisions.* Homewood, Ill.: Dow Jones–R. D. Irwin, 1972.

Granof, Michael H. *Financial Accounting: Principles and Issues.* Englewood Cliffs, N.J.: Prentice-Hall, 1977.

Perera, Phillips. *Development Finance: Institutions, Problems, and Prospects.* New York: Praeger, 1968.

Pidgeon, Guy W. *Financial Control in Developing Countries, with Particular Reference to State Corporations.* London: Longmans, 1971.

Pouliquen, Louis Y. *Risk Analysis in Project Appraisal.* World

Bank Staff Occasional Papers, no. 11. Baltimore: Johns Hopkins University Press, 1970.

Singhvi, Surendra S. *Corporate Financial Management in a Developing Economy.* International Business Series, Studies in Finance, no. 1. Seattle: University of Washington, 1972.

Spitler, Earl A. *Financial Accounting: Basic Concepts.* Homewood, Ill.: R. D. Irwin, 1977.

Welsch, Glenn A., and Robert N. Anthony. *Fundamentals of Financial Accounting.* Homewood, Ill.: R. D. Irwin, 1977.

Economic analysis

Anderson, Lee G., and Russell F. Settle. *Benefit-Cost Analysis: A Practical Guide.* Lexington, Mass.: Lexington Books, 1977.

Campbell, Rita R. *Food Safety Regulation: A Study of the Use and Limitations of Cost-Benefit Analysis.* Washington, D.C.: American Enterprise Institute for Public Policy Research, 1974.

Clifton, David S., and David E. Fyffe. *Project Feasibility Analysis.* New York: John Wiley and Sons, 1977.

Dasgupta, Ajit K., and D. W. Pearce. *Cost-Benefit Analysis: Theory and Practice.* New York: Barnes and Noble, 1972.

Frost, Michael J. *How to Use Cost-Benefit Analysis in Project Appraisal.* New York: John Wiley and Sons, 1975.

Gittinger, J. Price. *Economic Analysis of Agricultural Projects.* A World Bank Publication. 2d ed. Baltimore: Johns Hopkins University Press, 1979.

Hartmut, Schneider. *National Objectives and Project Appraisal in Developing Countries.* Washington, D.C.: Organization for Economic Co-operation and Development (OECD), 1975.

Lal, Deepak. *Methods of Project Analysis: A Review.* World Bank Staff Occasional Papers, no. 16. Baltimore: Johns Hopkins University Press, 1974.

Little, Ian, and J. A. Mirrlees. *Project Appraisal and Planning for Developing Countries.* New York: Basic Books, 1974.

Mishan, E. J. *Cost-Benefit Analysis.* New York: Praeger, 1976.

Ray, Anandarup, and Herman G. van der Tak. "A New Approach to the Economic Analysis of Projects." *Finance and Development,* vol. 16, no 1 (March 1979), pp. 28–32.

Roemer, Michael, and Joe Stern. *The Appraisal of Development Projects: A Practical Guide to Project Analysis, with Case Studies and Solutions.* New York: Praeger, 1975.

Scott, M., J. D. MacArthur, and D. M. G. Newberry. *Project Appraisal in Practice: The Little-Mirrlees Method Applied in Kenya.* London: Heinemann Educational Books, 1976.

Squire, Lyn, and Herman G. van der Tak. *Economic Analysis of Projects.* A World Bank Research Publication. Baltimore: Johns Hopkins University Press, 1975.

United Nations Industrial Development Organization (UNIDO). *Guidelines for Project Evaluation.* Sales no. 72.II.B.11. New York, 1972.

————. *Guide to Practical Project Appraisal: Social Benefit-Cost Analysis in Developing Countries.* Project Formulation and Evaluation Series, no. 3; Sales no. E.78.II.B.3. New York, 1978.

2. The Marketing Factor

Marketing research techniques

Albaum, Gerald S., and M. Venkatesan (eds.). *Scientific Marketing Research.* New York: Macmillan Free Press, 1971.

Ferber, Robert (ed.). *Handbook of Marketing Research.* New York: McGraw-Hill, 1974.

Green, Paul E., and Donald S. Tull. *Research for Marketing Decisions.* 3d ed. Englewood Cliffs, N.J.: Prentice-Hall, 1975.

————. *Research for Marketing Decisions.* 4th ed. Englewood Cliffs, N.J.: Prentice-Hall, 1978.

Kraemar, John. *Marketing Research in the Developing Countries.* New York: Praeger, 1971.

Kurtz, R. *Market Research Strategy and Techniques.* Braintree, Mass.: D. H. Mark Publishing Co., 1969.

Livingstone, James M. *A Management Guide to Market Research.* New York: Macmillan, 1977.

Luck, David J., Hugh G. Wales, and Donald A. Taylor. *Marketing Research.* 4th ed. Englewood Cliffs, N.J.: Prentice-Hall, 1974.

Schewe, Charles D. (ed.). *Marketing Information System: Selected Readings.* Chicago: American Marketing Association, 1976.

Market structure

Bain, Joe. *Industrial Organization.* New York: John Wiley and Sons, 1968.

Caves, Richard. *American Industry: Structure, Conduct, Performance*. Englewood Cliffs, N.J.: Prentice-Hall, 1972.

Food and Agriculture Organization (FAO). *Agricultural Marketing Boards*. Rome: FAO, 1974.

Hoos, Sidney (ed.). *Agricultural Marketing Boards: An International Perspective*. Cambridge, Mass.: Ballinger Publishing Co., 1979.

Porter, Michael. *Competitive Strategy: Techniques for Analyzing Business, Industry, and Competitors*. New York: Macmillan Free Press, 1980.

Shephard, William. *Market Power and Economic Welfare: An Introduction*. New York: Random House, 1970.

Marketing communications and development

Frey, Frederick W. "Communication and Development." In *Handbook of Communication*. Edited by Ithiel de Sola Pool and others. Chicago: Rand McNally College Publishing Co., 1973.

Lerner, Daniel. "Toward a Communication Theory of Modernization." In *Communications and Political Development*. Edited by Lucien W. Pye. Princeton: Princeton University Press, 1963.

Nielsen, Richard P. "Marketing and Development in LDC's." *Columbia Journal of World Business*, vol. 9, no. 4 (Winter 1974), pp. 46–49.

Rao, Y. U. Lakshmana. *Communications and Development: A Study of Two Indian Villages*. Minneapolis: University of Minnesota Press, 1963.

Rogers, Everett M., in association with Lynne Svenning. *Modernization among Peasants: The Impact of Communication*. New York: Holt, Rinehart & Winston, 1969.

UNIDO. "Expert Group Meeting on Marketing Management and Strategy for the Developing World." New York, 1975.

Competitive response

Heskett, James L. *Marketing*. New York: Macmillan, 1976. (See especially chapter 3.)

Porter, Michael. *Competitive Strategy*. (See under "Market structure," above.)

Rodger, Leslie W. *Marketing in a Competitive Economy*. 3d ed. New York: John Wiley and Sons, 1973.

Forecasting methods

Rao, Vithala R., and James E. Cox, Jr. *Sales Forecasting Methods: A Survey of Recent Developments.* Cambridge, Mass.: Marketing Science Institute (14 Story Street, Cambridge, Mass. 02138), 1978. (Literature review, including an annotated bibliography on sales forecasting.)

UNIDO. *Manual for the Preparation of Industrial Feasibility Studies* Sales no. E.78.II.B.5. New York, 1978. (See especially Annex VI on demand forecasting and Annex VII on market surveys.)

Export marketing

Basche, James R., Jr. *Export Marketing Services and Costs.* New York: The Conference Board, 1971.

Goldberg, Ray A. *Agribusiness Management in Developing Countries: Latin America.* Cambridge, Mass.: Ballinger Publishing Co., 1974.

Organization of American States (OAS), General Secretariat. *Methods for Evaluating Latin American Export Operations: A Manual for New Exporters.* Washington, D.C., 1978. (A guide to foreign market entry, sales collection, government regulations, forecasting, and financial and production planning and control.)

Slyper, Martin P. *Assessing Export Potential.* London: Gower Press, 1972.

Terpstra, Vern. *International Marketing.* 2d ed. Hinsdale, Ill.: Dryden Press, 1978.

Marketing management

Anderson, W. Thomas, Jr., Catherine Carlisle Bentley, and Louis K. Sharpe IV. *Multidimensional Marketing: Managerial, Societal, Philosophical.* Austin, Tex.: Austin Press, 1976.

Ball, Martin L. *Marketing Concepts and Strategy.* 3d ed. Boston: Houghton Mifflin, 1979.

Brannen, William H. *Successful Marketing for Your Small Business.* Englewood Cliffs, N.J.: Prentice-Hall, 1978.

Carman, James M., and Kenneth P. Whe. *Marketing: Principles and Methods.* 7th ed. Homewood, Ill.: R. D. Irwin, 1973.

Christopher, Martin, and Gordon Wells (eds.). *Marketing Logistics and Distribution Planning.* London: Allen and Unwin, 1972.

Davar, Rustom S. *Modern Marketing Management in the Indian Context*. Bombay: Progressive Corporation, 1969.

FAO. *Marketing Guides*. Rome; numbered, titled, and dated as follows:

  no. 1, "Marketing Problems and Improvement Programmes," 1975;

  no. 2, "Marketing Fruit and Vegetables," 2d ed., 1974;

  no. 3, "Marketing of Livestock and Meat," 2d ed., 1977;

  no. 4, "Marketing Eggs and Poultry," 4th printing, 1978;

  no. 6, "Rice Marketing," 1972;

  no. 7, "Fertilizer Marketing," 1976.

Heskett, James L. *Marketing*. (See "Competitive response," above.)

Kotler, Philip. *Marketing Decision-making: A Model-building Approach*. New York: Holt, Rinehart & Winston, 1971.

———. *Marketing Management: Analysis, Planning, and Control*. 3d ed. Englewood Cliffs, N.J.: Prentice-Hall, 1976.

Lazer, William, and Eugene J. Kelley (eds.). *Social Marketing: Perspectives and Viewpoints*. Homewood, Ill.: R. D. Irwin, 1973.

McCarthy, E. Jerome. *Basic Marketing; A Managerial Approach*. 5th ed. Homewood, Ill.: R. D. Irwin, 1975.

3. The Procurement Factor

Amihud, Yakov (ed.). *Conference on Bidding and Auctioning*. New York: New York University Press, 1976.

Baily, Peter J. H. *Purchasing and Supply Management*. 4th ed. London: Chapman and Hall, 1978.

Corey, E. Raymond. *Procurement Management: Strategy, Organization, and Decision-making*. Boston: CBI Publishing Co., 1978.

Guthrie, Thomas L., and James C. Snyder. *Procurement Planning for the Commercial Feed Farm*. Economic Research Service, U.S. Department of Agriculture. Washington D.C.: U.S. Government Printing Office, 1973.

Lee, L., and D. Dobler. *Purchasing and Material Management*. New York: McGraw-Hill, 1971.

New, Colin. *Requirements Planning*. New York: John Wiley and Sons, 1973.

United Nations. *A Guide to Industrial Purchasing*. ID/82; Sales no. 72.II.B.19. New York, 1972.

UNIDO. *UNIDO Guides to Information Sources.* New York; numbered, titled, and dated as follows:
  no. 1/rev. 1, "Meat Processing Industry," 1976;
  no. 3, "Leather and Leather Processing Industry," 1979;
  no. 4/rev. 1, "Furniture and Joinery Industry," 1977;
  no. 7/rev. 1, "Vegetable Oil Processing Industry," 1977;
  no. 11, "Pulp and Paper Industry," 1974;
  no. 12, "Clothing Industry," 1974;
  no. 15, "Non-alcoholic Beverage Industry," 1975;
  no. 19, "Canning Industry," 1975;
  no. 23, "Dairy Product Manufacturing Industry," 1976;
  no. 25, "Beer and Wine Industry," 1977;
  no. 27, "Packaging Industry," 1977;
  no. 28, "Coffee, Cocoa, Tea, and Spices," 1977.

4. The Processing Factor

Technology selection

Asian Productivity Organization. *International Subcontracting: A Tool of Technology Transfer.* Tokyo, 1978.

Bhalla, A. S. (ed.). *Technology and Employment in Industry.* Geneva: International Labour Office (ILO), 1975.

Chudson, Walter A., and Louis T. Wells, Jr. *The Acquisition of Proprietary Technology by Developing Countries from Multinational Enterprises: A Review of Issues and Policies.* New York: United Nations, Economic and Social Council (ECOSOC), June 1973.

Crane, Diane. *An Inter-organizational Approach to the Development of Indigenous Technological Capabilities: Some Reflections on the Literature.* OECD Development Center, Industry and Technology Occasional Papers, no. 3. Washington, D.C.: OECD, December 1974.

Darrow, Ken, and Rick Pam. *Appropriate Technology Sourcebook.* Stanford: Volunteers in Asia, November 1976.

Fitchett, Delbert A. "Capital-Labor Substitution in the Manufacturing Sector of Panama." *Economic Development and Cultural Change,* vol. 4, no. 3 (April 1976), pp. 577–92.

Ghandour, Marwan, and Jürgen Müller. "A New Approach to Technological Dualism." *Economic Development and Cultural Change*, vol. 27, no. 4 (July 1979), pp. 629–37.

Jequier, Nicholas (ed.). *Appropriate Technology: Problems and Promises*. Paris: OECD, 1976.

Keddie, James. "Adoptions of Production Techniques by Industrial Firms in Indonesia." Ph.D. dissertation. Cambridge, Mass.: Harvard University, 1975.

Lebell, Don, Konrad Schultz, and J. Fred Weston. "Small-scale Industries and Developing Countries." *California Management Review*, vol. 17, no. 1 (Fall 1974), pp. 32–40.

Lecraw, Donald J. "Choice of Technology in Low-wage Countries: The Case of Thailand." Ph.D. dissertation. Cambridge Mass.: Harvard University, 1976.

Lester, J. M. *Technology Transfer and Developing Countries: A Selected Bibliography*. Washington, D.C.: George Washington University, 1974.

Long, Frank. "A Basic Needs Strategy for Technology." *The American Journal of Economics and Sociology*, vol. 37, no. 3 (July 1978), pp. 261–70.

Morawetz, David. "Employment Implications of Industrialization in Developing Countries: A Survey." *The Economic Journal*, vol. 84, no. 335 (September 1974), pp. 491–542.

Pickett, James, D. J. C. Forsyth, and N. S. McBain. "The Choice of Technology, Economic Efficiency, and Employment in Developing Countries." *World Development*, vol. 2, no. 3 (March 1974), pp. 47–54.

Pratten, C. F. *Economies of Scale in Manufacturing Industry*. London: Cambridge University Press, 1971.

Schumacker, E. F. *Small Is Beautiful*. New York: Harper and Row, 1973.

Stewart, Francis. "Choice of Technique in Developing Countries." *Journal of Development Studies*, vol. 9, no. 1 (October 1972), pp 99–121.

Teitel, Simón. "Economies of Scale and Size of Plant: The Evidence and the Implications for the Developing Countries." *Journal of Common Market Studies*, vol. 13, nos. 1 and 2 (1975), pp. 92–115.

Timmer, C. P., and others. *The Choice of Technology in Developing Countries: Some Cautionary Tales*. Harvard Studies in International Affairs, no. 32. Cambridge, Mass.: Harvard University, Center for International Affairs, 1975. Processed.

United Nations. *Guidelines for the Acquisition of Foreign Technology in Developing Countries, with Special Reference to Technology Licence Agreements.* ID/98; Sale no. 73.II.B.1. New York, 1973.

————. Bureau of Economic Affairs. *Industrialization and Productivity.* Bulletin no. 2. New York, March 1959.

————. Conference on Trade and Development. *Handbook on the Acquisition of Technology by Developing Countries.* Sales no. E.78.II.D.15. New York, 1978.

UNIDO. *National Approaches to the Acquisition of Technology.* ID/187. New York, May 1977.

————. "Abstracts on Technology Transfer—Studies and Reports on the Development and Transfer of Technology (1970–76)." ID/189. New York, May 1977.

White, Lawrence J. "The Evidence on Appropriate Factor Proportions for Manufacturing in Less Developed Countries: A Survey." *Economic Development and Cultural Change,* vol. 27, no. 2 (December 1978), pp. 27–58.

Textile- and food-processing technology

Bhalla, A. S. "Investment Allocation and Technical Choice—A Case of Cotton-spinning Techniques." *The Economic Journal,* vol. 74, no. 295 (September 1964), p. 25.

Fennema, O. W., and others. *Low-temperature Preservation of Foods and Living Matter.* New York: Marcel Dekker, 1973.

Lund, D. "Heat Processing." In *Physical Principles of Food Preservation.* Edited by M. Kavel and others. New York: Marcel Dekker, 1975.

Pack, Howard. "The Optimality of Used Equipment: Calculations for the Cotton Textile Industry." *Economic Development and Cultural Change,* vol. 26, no. 2 (January 1978), pp. 307–25.

Peterson, M. S., and D. K. Tressler. *Food Technology the World Over.* Vol. 2. Westport, Conn.: Avi Publishing Co., 1965.

Tressler, D. K., and others (eds.). *The Freezing Preservation of Foods.* Vol. 1. Westport, Conn.: Avi Publishing Co., 1968.

Van Aredel, W. B., and M. J. Copley (eds.). *Food Dehydration.* Vol. 2. Westport, Conn.: Avi Publishing Co., 1964.

Williams, David. "National Planning and the Choice of Technology: The Case of Textiles in Tanzania." Ph.D. dissertation. Cambridge, Mass.: Harvard University, Graduate School of Business Administration, 1975.

Index

Advertising, 42, 128; promotion and, 50, 51, 52

Agrarian reform, 73, 74, 107

Agribusiness, project analysis and, 15–16

Agriculture, 11–12; agroindustries and, 6–7

Agrochemicals, 73, 86–87, 107

Agroindustrial projects: competitive environment and, 38–44; consumer analysis and, 29–38; cost and, 96–104; cycle stages of, 20–22; demand forecasting and, 59–67; inventory management and, 144–51; marketing analysis overview and, 27–29; marketing plan and, 45–57; plant location and, 138–43; processing technology and, 118–37; procurement system organization and, 105–14; programming and, 154–57; quality and, 85–89; quantity and, 71–83; supplies for processing and, 152–53; timing and, 90–95. See also Project analysis

Agroindustry: defining, 3–5; economic development and, 5–14; export generation and, 11–13; project analysis and, 15–19

Alcohol. See Ethanol; Gasohol

Anand Cooperative (India), 112

Animal feed, 81, 100. See also Livestock

Bates, Robert, 143

Biomass, 127–28

Brands: franchise, 42; promotion and, 51

Buying process, 34–35

By-products, 78, 95, 137, 158–60, 161; bagasse as, 159; checklist for, 198. See also Energy; Food processing

Canning, 153; comparison of equipment for, 176–77; cost estimates of, 162–65

Capacity: costs of idle, 145; use of, 128–29

Capital: inventory and, 149–51; labor and processing, 120–26; procurement and, 109

Carbohydrates, processing and, 130

Causal demand forecasting models, 64–65

Cereals, storage and, 146–47

Chaya, 30

Chenery, Hollis B., 8

Collective organizations, 109–12

Compañía Nacional de Subsistencias Populares (CONASUPO), 35, 111

Competition, 68; basis of, 39–42; checklist for, 179–80; distribution and, 57–58; identification of, 38–39; institutional constraints and, 43–44; prices and, 39–40, 42; raw materials and, 79–83

Consumer analysis, 29–37, 68; checklist for, 178–79; quality and, 85

Contracting, 101–02

Corporations (transnational), 24

Cost estimates, 162–65

Costs, 161; backward integration and, 103, 109; checklist for, 189–91; determinants of procurement, 97–101; disadvantage of absolute, 42; idle capacity and, 145; inventory and, 149–51; land, 142–43; pricing mechanisms and, 101–03; yield determinations and, 76–77

Crops: consumption and, 80–81; insect damage to, 89, 146, 147, 157; losses of, 82–83; mix of, procurement and, 107; required area for

development planning and, 23–24, 143; plant location and, 142; project profitability and, 23; research and, 23; subsidies and, 43–44

Handling, 121; losses from, 83; quality and, 87–88
Hoffman, Walter D., 8

Identification of projects, 20–21
Implementation plans, 21, 154–55
Imports, 43, 153
Import substitution, 8
Incomes policies, 23
Industrialization (rural), 6–7
Industrial sector, 30; agroindustrial project analysis and, 14–15
Infant formulas, 34, 50–51
Inflation, 23
Infrastructure, 111; plant location and, 140–42; public sector, 22; rural, 6
Inputs (farm), 111; quality and, 86–87; usage of, 73–74
Institute of Food Product Research and Development (Thailand), 136–37
Institutional constraints, 43–44
Integration, 153; backward, 103; backward vertical, 108–09, 116; forward vertical, 112; vertical, 115
Inter-American Development Bank (IDB), 14
International Finance Corporation (IFC), 14
International trade, 22
Inventory management, 144–51, 156; checklist for, 196
Irrigation, 107

Judgmental demand estimates, 62

Labor, 161; capital/processing and, 120–26; cost estimates and, 162; plant location and, 140
Lamson-Scribner, Frank H., 140
Land, market analysis and, 29
Land costs, plant location and, 142–43, 161
Land ownership, 107
Land tenure, 74
Land-use patterns, 71–73
Legumes, storage and, 148
Licensing, 44

Linkages: agribusiness, 15; backward, 7
Livestock, 73, 74, 86, 93; crop use and, 81; damaged grain and, 147; seasonality and, 90

Machinery. See Equipment
Managerial resources, 129
"M&S Equipment Cost Index," 162
Manufacturing sector, 7–11
Marketing analysis: barriers to entry and, 42, 44; competitive environment and, 38–44; consumer analysis and, 29–38; demand forecasting and, 59–67; marketing plan and, 45–57; overview of, 27–29; plant location and, 138–40
Marketing associations, 53
Marketing mix, 56, 68
Marketing plan, 49–57, 69; buying process and, 34; checklist for, 180–83; pricing strategies and, 47–49; product design and, 45–47
Marketing research. See Research, marketing
Marketing studies, 21
Market segmentation, 30–34
Market structure, competition and, 38–39
Meat processing, 81, 139; poultry, 99–100, 158–59; beef, 106, 110, 141–42
Meat products: sanitary standards and, 43; storage and, 148
Middlemen, 98
Milling, 6, 91, 118–19, 120–21; processing and, 131–36; storage and, 147
Minerals, processing and, 131
Monetary policies, 23

Nutritional issues, 13, 26, 98, 157; crop changes and, 72; crop consumption and, 80; fortification and, 136–37; fruit and vegetable processing and, 136; harvesting and, 87; marketing and, 30, 31; milling and, 131–36; minerals/processing and, 131; perishability and, 91; promotion and, 50–51; proteins/carbohydrates/fats and, 130; storage and, 88, 146–47, 148–49; supply sources and, 153; technological effect on, 129–31; vitamins/processing and, 130–31

James E. Austin is professor at the Harvard Graduate School of Business Administration, a lecturer at the Harvard School of Public Health, and a consultant and visiting lecturer at the Economic Development Institute of the World Bank.

The full range of World Bank publications, both free and for sale, is described in the *Catalog of World Bank Publications*; the continuing research program is outlined in *World Bank Research Program: Abstracts of Current Studies*. Both booklets are updated annually; the most recent edition of each is available without charge from the Publications Unit, World Bank, 1818 H Street, N.W., Washington, D.C. 20433, U.S.A.